T0278041

Praise for *Collisions of Earth and Sky*

"*Collisions of Earth and Sky* is an existential exploration of the human relationship with nature and what it really means to develop a sense of place. Part poetry, part manifesto, Barr's writing is a bold rejection of the culture and policies that have alienated humans from the natural world. I haven't read anything like it in the nature connection genre. Ultimately, she challenges us to find our deepest selves by making space for the wild in our lives, and shows that we are better off for it."

—**Linda Åkeson McGurk**, author of *There's No Such Thing as Bad Weather* and *The Open-Air Life*

"These days, faith no longer moves mountains. No such Herculean chores are required for today's challenges. A stranger faith, like music, filters through the prisms of permanence and human exceptionality, whispering tunes from pine cones, restless rivers, and elder hills. A stranger religion. A beautiful collision. This tune wants us to listen, to dance. If you have ever had your ears stolen by a wild longing, if you have ever sought a grander healing, let the caress of Heidi Barr's words and rhapsodies sway you toward the magic of the world wild and alive."

—**Bayo Akomolafe, PhD**, author of *These Wilds Beyond Our Fences: Letters to My Daughter on Humanity's Search for Home* and host of the course and festival series We Will Dance with Mountains

"Heidi Barr's latest work, *Collisions of Earth and Sky*, is indeed that—a collision. A confluence of ideas and feelings, excavations of the past and hope for the future. It isn't exactly what one might expect from your typical book about the healing power of nature. It is indeed that, but it also doesn't shy away from honest reflections about the author's history, as well as our shared history, a history that includes ugliness as well as beauty. As a good writer, a good healer, a good *excavator*, she digs it all up and, in doing so, offers us a pathway to healing in the future—one that doesn't neglect our place in the historical and ecological web of relationships."

—**Theodore Richards**, founder of The Chicago Wisdom
Project and author of *The Great Re-Imagining:
Spirituality in an Age of Apocalypse* and
Reimagining the Classroom

"Heidi Barr's writing always feels like a gentle but persistent invitation to slow my body, mind, and breath, to look up, to feel deeply, and to live fully present in what is. In *Collisions of Earth and Sky* I feel the truth of our interconnectedness deep in my bones and in the steadiness of my heartbeat. My body knows well that to be human is both grief and beauty, a tangle of questions to dance with, not an experience to tidy up. When we allow ourselves to be broken open enough to feel the bite of cold on our weary bodies, to tell the full truth of our longing and despair, to carefully hold each other's stories, then we practice hope in action. And hope in action is the only kind of hope I'm interested in."

—**Krista O'Reilly-Davi-Digui**, holistic embodiment
coach and joyful living educator

"While reading this wellspring of wisdom, it was like sitting at my mother's kitchen table drinking in her *dichos de mi madre*. These 'impossibly beautiful' contemplative insights are what is needed to heal the universe."

—**Aimée Medina Carr**, author of *River of Love*

"Heidi Barr has done it again! Reading *Collisions of Earth and Sky* feels like taking a refreshing meander through the woods with a time-tested friend, swapping stories and remembering our true selves. Barr invites us to join her in asking curious and reverent questions, then listening deeply to nature, each other, and ourselves, returning to our creatureliness. This book is a gift in its gentle and profound path to a mindful pace and intentionality, allowing the wildness of life to unfold in and around us."

—**Ellie Roscher**, author of *The Embodied Path*

"Using her prairie poet's sentience and acuity, Heidi Barr offers us an engaging long-form work which is an invitation to deeper and more authentic self-knowing. She uses the natural world as a framework and guides us toward attentiveness and into fuller ways of engaging our surroundings and ourselves. Step into this journey!"

—**Lisa Colón DeLay**, host of the *Spark My Muse* podcast and author of *The Wild Land Within*

COLLISIONS
of EARTH
and SKY

COLLISIONS of EARTH and SKY

CONNECTING WITH NATURE FOR NOURISHMENT, REFLECTION, AND TRANSFORMATION

HEIDI BARR

Broadleaf Books

Minneapolis

COLLISIONS OF EARTH AND SKY
Connecting with Nature for Nourishment, Reflection, and Transformation

Cover image: Getty Images/breath10
Cover design: Olga Grlic

Print ISBN: 978-1-5064-8254-5
eBook ISBN: 978-1-5064-8255-2

*For all of those who see their reflection
in the shadow of the mountain*

A Land Acknowledgment

I'm going to start this with another acknowledgment—that while a land acknowledgment is an important step on the road toward collective global healing and decolonization, it's just that: one (very small) step. Any land acknowledgment must be followed by many, many more steps, and they must include tangible real-world action. It's also worth noting that, according to Dr. Len Necefer (founder of NativesOutdoors), most land acknowledgments lack nuance. They typically do not reflect all the differing ways that various tribes view land ownership (for example, the common westernized view of "stolen land" doesn't work as well when a group of people believes that they belong to the land, not that the land belongs to them). They also often oversimplify beliefs by focusing *only* on land (for example, for some Indigenous groups, water or dreams hold more cultural significance than the land does).

So what follows is one small, imperfect step in what I hope is the right direction. Then one of my next steps is to ensure that 50 percent of author royalties from this book are passed on to Indigenous-run organizations, especially those in Minnesota, South Dakota, and western Wisconsin.

The land that sustains me today has been stewarded by Indigenous people for thousands of years. The words you'll be reading in this book were primarily put to paper or typed out in eastern Minnesota, or Mni Sota Makhoche, which, when translated from Dakota into English, means "land where water reflects the sky," on the ancestral and contemporary lands stewarded by the Wahpekute, part of the Dakota Nation, lands that also hold historical and contemporary significance to the Ojibwe and the Ho-Chunk. At present, eleven Indigenous Nations—four Dakota communities in the south and seven Ojibwe communities in the north—are federally recognized in the state of Minnesota. A great many more Dakota, Ojibwe, and other Native American folks reside in communities and cities throughout the state as well. Some of it was also written in South Dakota, both east and west of the Missouri River— Mnišoše in Lakota—on ancestral and contemporary lands stewarded by the Oceti Šakowiŋ. (Oceti Šakowiŋ means the Seven Council Fires, which is the historic alliance of seven divisions of the groups that have also been called the Sioux.) There are nine federally recognized nations in the state of South Dakota today, and many Santee-Dakota, Yankton-Nakota, and Teton-Lakota folks live throughout the state. Due to colonization (both historical and ongoing), forced removal, and genocide—much of which was carried out by the US government as a way to acquire land—many Indigenous people have been disconnected from their ancestral homelands. As the Native Governance Center in St. Paul, Minnesota, says, "Indigenous people are not relics of the past." Rather, Indigenous people are still here, and their continual and important contributions to society need to be acknowledged and celebrated.

To learn more about the land you are on, visit https://native-land.ca/. Some ways of supporting Indigenous folks, if you need ideas (no matter where you are located), include donating time, money, and resources (especially to Indigenous-led initiatives), amplifying Native American voices, and returning (or advocating for the returning of) land.[1]

May our daily practice, despite its messiness and mistakes, be grounded in working toward a decolonized world, where all humans, creatures, land, waters, and spiritual beliefs are treated with respect.

Contents

CONTENTS

We are coming to a time of listening.
Our sweat and breath are now upon the land.
Voices rise up, and we begin to hear the echoes in the stones.[1]

—KENT NERBURN

Preface

There and Back Again

The plane touched down on the arid shores of Malta in January 2001. Six months of island living stretched out before me on the blue Mediterranean horizon. The World Trade Center towers still stood. The euro had yet to come into being. There were internet cafés mixed in with the shops providing dial-up service. Cell phones were not yet common, and I had a camera that used film that had to be developed. The world was about to pick up its speed of change rapidly. A college junior, I'd left a series of confusing relationships behind in America, and I had no idea what I wanted to do after graduation. I was in a place of deep uncertainty. It felt like something was missing, but I wasn't sure what that something was. Going to Malta seemed like part of the answer to the questions I didn't yet know how to ask.

After growing up surrounded by a sea of grass on the South Dakota prairie, a sea of deep blue saltwater was thrilling. It captured my attention during that unmoored time. I discovered those deep blue waters had many moods, from calm and serene to churning and angry to singing songs of enchantment. My flatmates and I lived in Sliema, an urban, tourist-driven community right on the water's edge. We could see more concrete than anything else when we threw open our fourth-floor window, but the sea was just down the street and around the corner. The sheer volume of nearby water somehow kept me grounded—in a different way than the prairie of my youth but grounded nonetheless. The sea reminded me (a reminder I often wasn't fully conscious of at the time) that life needs to be lived with intention to feel true and that feelings need to be felt no matter how much they hurt. It reminded me that I felt more alive when I paid attention to the wild undercurrents of the world.

Most of those six months were spent in a haze of alcohol, lying in the sun and untangling myself from the sorts of young adulthood dramas that arise when six to eight twentysomethings share a living space and there's a pub within throwing distance in both directions. The rest of the time was spent writing papers, learning about other cultures, and maintaining passing grades in the university classes required for graduation. I had to figure out how to partner with the colliding forces in my life instead of fighting or ignoring them. It was my first foray into figuring out how to live my life in a way that tells the truth.

Around another corner from our flat was a little nook carved out in a row of old stone buildings—just enough room for a very old woman and her boxes of blood oranges, vegetables, and flowers to set up shop. She was there nearly every week. Visiting her to get an orange was kind of like visiting the sea. It was grounding. Her way of being brought me straight to the here and now. She reminded me how life could be lived: with intention and the sort of patience that has the power to last eight decades, even as tourism ate up the little available farmland on the island and young people started to buy their groceries from the bigger shops in the next town over. She demonstrated that it was still possible to choose where to put one's energy, even if the way forward doesn't seem to present much choice or the path toward what to do is unclear. She invited me to consider what else could be possible.

The world shifted further shortly after I returned to America. The Twin Towers fell. Fear of "the other" continued to grow. The pace of technology continued to quicken. I graduated from college, found a job, got married, and had a child. Through all that change, I held on to a rock I picked up one day on a windblown beach. During those island days, I'd taken to carrying it with me. The sea had beaten it down. It was full of pockmarks, scratches, and indentations. The rock had holes, yes, but they were openings to fill up with wholeness. It was the embodiment of what can happen when elemental forces collide.

Many people whom I have known, and many whom I still know, are searching for something—that thing that is going to make them happy, that idea that will tip the scales in the direction of abundance, that significant other who will make them feel like they matter. I have been this person, too, and certainly was during those six months in Malta. Over the past several years, I've been able to come to a place inside myself that allows me to see more clearly than I once did, at least most of the time. Not always. The journey isn't ever really over, even when you come home again. It simply evolves. The old woman and the sea showed me that we have the capacity to handle what happens even if we wash up on unfamiliar shores, even if the journey leaves deep marks. The marks leave us more beautiful, more filled with depth and texture than before. This doesn't mean our lives are without hardship or pain or unfulfilled needs. Yet those perceived holes provide space to evolve. Those holes help us build the capacity to remember the wholeness that we have always had.

I went across the ocean and back again, and though I didn't recognize it while it was happening, that journey expanded my awareness of myself and the world. An elder, the sea, a blood orange, and a rock were all unlikely teachers along the way, but they were part of my becoming. They were partners in the dance of living that helped me find my way, through collisions of earth and sky.

Introduction

If I had to name the thing I've become the *most* proficient at during my career as a health and wellness coach, I'd have to say it's asking questions. In the world of behavior change, we throw around terms like *appreciative inquiry* and *motivational interviewing* in workplace conversation, and we answer questions from clients like "What should I do next?" with "What are your best options?" Over the years, I've found that many folks don't like to be told what to do, even if they ask for advice. A strategically placed question in a hard conversation can open doors that might otherwise remain closed. Reflection is quite often more impactful than being handed a solution, even if the answer doesn't come right away or the solution ends up being different than anticipated.

On good days, I call myself a wellness coach-turned-writer. I wake up feeling like I have something of value to contribute to the world, and I figure out how to put words together in a way that makes sense to other people. I pull those powerful questions out of the ether and elicit a response from a client that helps them move forward. I enjoy the work, and if it's hard, it's hard in a way that makes me want to keep at it. On less good days, I wake up feeling like I have run out of ideas, that my well of words has run dry. That I've used up my voice and my inquiry muscles have atrophied beyond rejuvenation. I wonder how I ever thought of all of those sentences and ideas and questions, and I imagine what life will be like now that I no longer have anything to say or ask.

Fortunately, those little negativity gremlins are always quelled by a new idea or when something else to get curious about turns up. Being alive has a way of providing material, whether I like that material or not. When I opt to head outside, instead of staring at the computer screen waiting for inspiration to strike, I find a way forward. Something more always comes since life on a living earth is never stagnant, even when it feels like it is. There are always more questions.

Research has indicated that spending time in a natural setting provides a plethora of benefits from lower blood pressure to increased immunity to an enhanced sense of well-being and happiness. Folks who appreciate nature tend to experience more moments of happiness, enjoy a more robust sense of well-being, and are more innovative. It's hard to hold on to the tension of a hectic day at work or from caregiving at home when you are lying in the grass, looking up at the sky. Spending time in natural light helps the body take in vitamin D, an essential building block of human health. Turning away from the computer screen to gaze at the horizon as the sun sinks into the westerly hills reminds us that we are part of something bigger and more profound than our everyday worries. We remember that there is beauty in the world outside our urban jungles, consumer economy, and humanmade inventions.

In short, being connected to nature helps us be more fully human and better planetary citizens. That connection can help us more effectively grapple with all the questions that come from being alive on Planet Earth. Time spent close to nature is a chance for nourishment, a call to right action, and an opportunity to reflect (among many other things) all rolled into one.

The work that I do, as both a writer and a wellness coach, is rooted in the idea that it's possible to notice beauty in the ordinary and in the wilds of the world, even when that beauty sits alongside the different ways devastation forces its hand on too many forms of life. It's the work of telling the truth as I see it unfolding in my own life and asking others what truths they see in theirs. Many of the other writers I know have said something along the lines of "I write because I can't not write." I can claim the same sentiment: Writing is a way of wrestling with what's going on in my own head, in my community, and on the planet. It's a way of figuring out how I truly feel about something and putting my introverted and soft-spoken voice out into the world. Part of my story is writing about what I notice and sharing it. Another part of my story is asking questions to help others discern what's true for them so they can claim their own story.

It feels important to say that I am not an expert or a seasoned researcher, and the internal biases that I have may well become apparent to those who look through a different lens than I do. My understanding of the world, and the world itself, will have evolved in the months between submitting the final draft for publication and publication day. This book is about what I have noticed by actively seeking truth in a very complicated world and being intentional about acknowledging my place in it. It's about the messy and imperfect ways that humans interact with each other and their land base, and it's about how living a life steeped in nature can offer hope and solace in times of despair and grief. It's about how owning our creatureliness, our wild nature, can help us live well. It's about how self-inquiry can lead to otherwise unexplored paths. I don't have all the answers. Sometimes I wonder if I have any answers at all, but one thing I know for sure is that we all have an origin. This human life is a journey, and we all return, at some point, to earth.

The journey tends to take up a lot of our energy—it's tempting to just "get there already." The idea of moving forward is a driver for many of us. But when we strip it down, a human life is a collection of present moments. Perhaps the purpose of the journey is to figure out what it means to exist in one's fullest version of truth. Life's work, you might say. We all have a unique way of being that is life-giving for ourselves, our communities, and this planet we share. We can cultivate the capacity to respond to whatever happens while we are alive in a way that serves us well, even though we are born into a life situation over which we have little control. Some of us have a much easier time of it than others; privilege is a very real force in our world, and it's one that perpetuates inequality and harm on a daily basis for a great many groups of people. Life is lost every day because of systemic racism, misogyny, and homophobia. Yet despite that inequity, do all human beings, somewhere inside when everything external is stripped away, have the capacity to look at the world through a lens of joyful enough-ness rather than one of scarcity and lack? I think so. But systemic change is direly needed. I have the time and resources, and quite possibly this perspective, to write these words down because I have what I need to survive largely because of the life situation I was born into. Those who have little and can find the joy in what they have are some of my greatest teachers.

My life today is punctuated by the in-between: my family grows much of our own food, and my father and two of my brothers are organic vegetable farmers who like to share, but we remain dependent on grocery stores, our neighbors, and regular paychecks to meet all of our needs. Our heat in winter comes partly from a woodburning stove, and we harvest downed wood from the land for fuel, yet with a 1970s-era split level that wasn't built with a woodstove in mind, we still need to use oil and electricity when it gets really cold. I'd love to say my lifestyle is all peaceful contemplation, foraging for wild edibles, raising my child, and advocating for social change, but there's plenty more that goes on around here that requires time and energy. I spend a fair amount of that energy doing what I feel called to do, like gardening, walking in the woods, writing, and being present with loved ones, but a full-time desk job still takes up more time than I find ideal. (Maybe you can relate.) My spouse and I both rely on the internet and computer technology to do the work that makes us each a paycheck. For a while there, our daughter needed that technology, too, for school during pandemic distance learning. We keep one television in the basement, and though I haven't turned it on more than a handful of times in the last several years, I know more about what's on Netflix than I care to admit. (Well, I guess I did just admit it.) We do our best to not let devices take up too much space in life. Some days are better than others.

As humans, our lifestyles are in constant evolution, filled with trial and error, beauty and destruction. We are continually breathing into the space that exists in between where we are and where we want to be. If I've learned anything from life so far, it is that there is no arriving—there is only the journey and being fully present for it. Which sometimes feels like a battle.

When I can stop fighting with myself, I find I'm living in a way that feels right because I am able to root fully in my life instead of trying to force an outcome that I think I should want. Yielding to what wants to speak through me has allowed me to tell the stories that want to be told. It's helped me ask others the questions that might help them tell their own. I am far from having things all figured out; I often hesitate and wonder if what I'm trying to say makes sense to anyone (including myself). I fall back into that internal battle more than I'd like to admit. Continuing to put energy into being present for the journey and allowing for course correction helps. Remembering that I am always returning to the parts of my origin that make me who I am helps. Connecting to nature helps. All of these things help me live the best life I can, even during hard times. All of these things help me find my way when powerful forces collide.

When earth and sky collide, it's a dance older than time. That collision illuminates possibilities for healing the parts of the world that are wounded: from the hugely global (like that which has been ravaged by colonization) to the hyper local (like personal frustration with perceived imperfections) to everything in between.

One late-spring day in the 1980s, my brothers and I found a weathered and rounded arrowhead in the field behind the house. (If I knew where it was today, I'd return it to the descendants of its makers.) Until the 1850s, the land on which the house I grew up in sits was home to the upper bands of the Dakota Nation. According to the historical marker that can be seen in the distance from my parents' driveway, in 1851, all land east of the Big Sioux River was acquired by the US government. As European immigrants and settlers began staking claims on lands across the American plains and further west, the landscape began changing. Origin, journey, and returning got all jumbled up as colonization made itself known on South Dakota and Minnesota soil.

The land where my childhood home sits gave my transplanted German and Norwegian personal roots a place to grow and be nourished. A place to interact with the wildness that is still the undercurrent of the world. I hope the land I am steward of now, in Minnesota, will give my daughter's roots the same nourishment. The land holds stories I will never know, as well as many that I can learn if I'm willing to listen and dig deeper than is comfortable. When I live grounded in my creatureliness and let nature inform my choices, I live the version of my life that feels the most real.

The pages that follow are a bit of a winding trail, full of opportunities for self-inquiry and reflection. It's a trail that meanders through myriad topics and landscapes, and it's one that is full of questions. I hope you, my fellow traveler on this journey of living, will move a few more steps toward more fully embracing your own creatureliness, your own place in this great web we all share, and let that be a foundation even when there are more questions than answers.

Perhaps you'll even discover a few things you didn't know were missing by hiking with me through these pages. I hope, through truth telling and having compassion for yourself and your fellow beings, that you'll find your own way to live the questions—with nature as your guide. Because when we let nature inform that self-inquiry and reflect on what comes up when we do, little by little, we uncover the parts of ourselves that can best contribute to the healing of the world.

The Invitation to Dance with Mountains

I often wonder what it would be like to dance with mountains. To sway with the majestic alpine wildflowers that dot the valleys or to listen to the whisper of clear snowmelt as it cascades to lower ground over a bed of stones smoothed to perfection. To kiss pine needles or to breathe the mysterious scent of ancient bedrock. I wonder what it would be like to mourn or prepare the dead or sit shiva in communion with earthy loam or lichen. To walk in step with the peaks that have been stripped of life, the woodlands that have been clear-cut, the toxic rivers, the fracked tundra, the topsoil that can't hold on. I often find myself wondering how cruelty, choices that hurt others, and hate can coexist with grace, goodness, and love. Is it possible to hold space for them all and hear what they have to say? These are my questions. Perhaps some of these are your questions too. You surely have plenty of your own.

"Dance with mountains."[1] *Sometimes I hear the wind whispering an invitation to dance with mountains as it blows outside my windows or when I'm walking to the mailbox.*

I am so often in the garden or the woods, at work, at home, at the grocery store but at the same time absent. Physically present but mentally checked out, worried, lamenting, even laughing, wondering what's next. I am searching for validation in this human experience but not sure what that even means. Can you relate? *Validation* is one of those chameleon words, a word that takes on different meanings all the time. I don't want to need validation, but it's one of those things that we humans crave. Acknowledgment matters. It's easy to listen to others, validate their experiences, and encourage them to feel what they feel and be present to each moment but harder to be on the other side. It can be scary to make the changes that are essential for living in a way that feels attuned to what your soul truly wants or what the world truly needs. I've been working on being in my present story in a way that is rooted in the more beautiful world: by paying attention to what my neighbors are going through and helping when I can, by not putting my own emotional needs last all the time, by taking steps to walk more lightly on the earth. Some days it feels like it will be a constant struggle. I get tired easily but can sense the turning of my face to the beauty that is still possible.

There it is again. "Dance with mountains."

We are not moving from here to there; we are making *here* and *there* by moving.

We are here to disrupt the stories we feel stuck within. We are learning a different definition of urgency.

We are walking with a foot in two different worlds.

To recover is to take on a new shape. We have to go to the edges of our skin.

The self is that which we haven't met yet. But somehow it's always been inside us.

We have an origin, but we don't always know it. Is it wild?

What if where we come from doesn't fit who we are now?

How do we find the courage to stand still enough to find the path?

How do we find the courage to move toward right action?

"Dance with mountains."

Who am I? Who are you?

Can this question even be answered? What is a person, really? A physical body, a set of cells and tissue. Skin a certain hue, hair a certain texture, body a certain size and shape. A way of thinking, of feeling, of loving, of existing alongside others. Sadness to joy to pain to exuberance. A bunch of stuff all wrapped up in a living creature. We're assigned a gender at birth, but it might not fit, or maybe it's changed. We are a relative or a partner or a child or a friend. We are lovers of nature, gardens, villages, cities, technology, books, mountains, deserts, prairies, rivers, soil. Some of us don't know what to do with ourselves in a big group and like to be alone. Some of us like constant companionship. All of us benefit from loving relationships and close communities. You and I, we are a paradox. We are on the earth, but sometimes we float above where we think we are as worry or lament or projection claims precious energy. We are souls, the wild part of the self that can't really be defined but that can be sensed as something greater than what we give ourselves credit for. Something that is the earth, that is the universe, that is the cosmos experiencing life in a human body. We are everything and nothing, all that is beautiful and haunting and destructive and healing.

"Dance with mountains." The wind is picking up. It's growing more persistent.

We are creatures on a planet, part of the earth's body. I, for one, feel unsure a lot, full of questions—but at the same time, I'm sure beyond any doubt that I am one small part of a bigger whole. Part of the rivers that flow through broken land. Part of the mountains that rise up and get beaten down and rise up again. Part of the delicate beauty of a translucent wildflower. Part of the steamrolling culture that so often swiftly decimates that which took millions of years to come into being. Part of the curious, the confused, the reckless, the patient. Part of peace and part of war. Part of the sword and part of the wound. Part of the beautiful, part of the ugly. Part of the fabric of this great web.

"Dance with mountains." Even on calm days, it's there.

Sometimes I feel haunted by what it takes to maintain a lifestyle that feels like it adequately supports my family. I know some folks are haunted by the false expectation that whatever is needed to sustain their current lifestyle must be done, others by always being the one who asks, "What do you need from me?" Some are haunted by easy choices and the challenge of simplifying. So many are haunted by the ghosts of white supremacy. By the realities of white supremacy. Some days I feel haunted by the shadows of mountains that want me to make different choices that are not yet clear.

"Dance with mountains."

But how? How do you think we find it within this human life to accept such an invitation? I invite you to imagine yourself so attuned to the natural world that you could waltz or swing dance with an ancient pile of rock and earth. To live so fully in your creatureliness that you could communicate with the world in a way that makes the sky weep in understanding and the plains shiver with anticipation at what is possible when life chooses harmony over dissonance. I invite you to think about what it would mean to identify the parts of yourself that are akin to rivers and hilltops and soil and trees. To truly listen to those who are different and act in ways that will make a difference. Somehow I know that there must be a way to hold that connection close to the bone and let it be a foundation. Imagine with me what it would be like to accept the invitation.

What would it be like to dance with mountains?

Part One

Origin

or·i·gin

ˈôrəjən/

noun

the point or place where something begins, arises, or is derived

We all have an origin, a place we started becoming—a base energy. Where we come from. Where we *originate*. As Aimée Medina Carr writes, "Our ancestors work through us; we are all walking family trees."[1] Most faith traditions and cultures have origin stories or myths: everyone comes from somewhere. We all come into being on the same planet, but we experience life differently. For many of us, the specific details of our origin are unknowable, and we may never learn the names of the people who walked generations before us, but we can still connect to our roots. Our shared origin is a living earth that's part of the universe that holds everyone. We aren't born into circumstances that provide equal footing for all as we evolve. We can't choose where we come from, but we can excavate what we need to rise into the realest versions of ourselves.

Origin is a mystery as much as it is seared into our bones.

Where I Come From

Where do you come from?

I come from green grass and big bluestem,
mountain streams and old log cabins,
winding rivers and geese that fly south,
returning again year after year.
I come from creatures who breathe,
swim and dance, sleep and howl
in the company of old red pines,
oak savannas and rocky ledges.
I come from anxiety and peace,
turbulent cascades and smooth waters,
gusty winds and the eye of the storm.
I come from all that is myth and magic,
wild and wandering,
rooted and real.
I come from destruction and healing,

across vast waters
and beyond open plains.
I come from quiet walks, hand in hand,
solitude and communion,
praise and lamentation.
I come from joy,
from sorrow,
from recognition there's so much I don't know.

Digging for the Truth

What truths come out when you dig into your cultural or familial history?

Moody County, South Dakota, 1991

Standing at the highest point as far as the eye can see, I gaze down the slope, skis aimed downward. Pushing off, I gradually build up speed, and for a few seconds, I feel like an Olympic racer conquering the super-G course. Crouching lower, I tuck my poles under my arms for the grand descent. Halfway down, I hit a clump of grass and fall in a tangled heap of arms, legs, poles, and old-school Nordic skis. Because the mountain that I was just careening down isn't in the Alps or even the foothills of the Rockies. It's in the cow pasture across the road from my childhood home on the prairie of South Dakota, and instead of scrubby pines and alpine bluebells, the base of this slope come spring is covered in big bluestem and pasque flowers. At twelve years old, this is my mountain.

My mother's side of the family can trace lineage back for eight generations, and the line never leaves the country of Germany. Seven generations back, the same name even appears on both sides of the tree. Avid travelers, my grandparents visited and researched and documented quite extensively, and the guest room in their home sported a full wall of photo albums and boxes of old slides to prove it. They visited the old "family castle" that's now a fancy yet ramshackle place to store hay in northern Germany and looked up countless relatives, and my grandfather had aspirations of writing a book about their discoveries. He died before this could come into being, but I have memories of him sitting at a boxy home computer in the late 1980s, peering through square-rimmed glasses at a black screen with square text and a blinking yellow cursor. There's a handy chart outlining the family tree that's been photocopied so every relative can have one. After coming to the United States just after the turn of the century to 1900, my grandparents' grandparents landed in southern Indiana.

My father's side of the family is not as well charted, but he does know his mother's side was 100 percent German, probably millers. And recently he and some cousins discovered the area in Norway that his great-great-grandfather left when he came to America. It's likely that he was a farmer in the old country, and based on some findings in that town, it's speculated there may have been a Viking settlement there in earlier times. There is an unwed mother (the scandal!) somewhere in the mix, making tracking the family name more complicated. But we know my father's great-grandfather settled in southwestern Minnesota when he was around forty years old, near what is now Blue Mound State Park. After a string of hardships befell the farm, his suicide and the allure of better times pulled the remaining family farther west, deep into the South Dakota prairie. I imagine their transition from Europe to America was filled with hope, struggle, sadness, uncertainty, and determination to find a place to call home.

My origin, in a genetic sense, is Germanic and northern European—what has now been homogenized on a census survey into the classification of "white." My ancestors came from a far-off land across the sea, soil that I have never touched and salty air that I have never smelled.

Most of my childhood was spent in a university town, and there was a population of students and faculty from other parts of the world, but by and large, I interacted with people whose ancestors were living somewhere in Europe as recently as a handful of generations ago. I had a few classmates at my public school who wouldn't have selected "white" on a survey, but not many.

The midwestern American slice of the Great Plains where I grew up is the homeland of many Indigenous Nations. I don't pretend to have familiarity with the customs of these people whose ancestors were here long before mine decided to board a ship to sail across the ocean from Scandinavia and Germany, but I do have great respect for their commitment to and spiritual connection with the land as well as for their resiliency. I was born on the Great Plains, but I'm the great-great-granddaughter of immigrants. My body wants to claim the prairie as its origin, but I don't know if I can do that—my ancestors were part of the immigrant wave that swept this land out from under the people who were already living on it. Doreen Manual said, during the book launch event for *Red Nation Rising*,[1] "I don't think people who don't come from this land can have the same relationship with the land that we do." If I'm being honest, that's not what I wanted to hear; there are times when I feel like this land is as much a part of who I am as the blood that runs through my veins. But the fact remains that there are people whose ancestors were here first.

Wendell Berry, an author whose work has been woven into my life since my folks had dinner with him and his wife at his farm in Kentucky in 1982, says it well in his essay "A Native Hill":

> I am forever being crept up on and newly startled by the revelation that my people established themselves here by killing or driving out the original possessors, by the awareness that people were once bought and sold here by my people, by the sense of violence they have done to their own kind and to each other and to the earth, by their persistent failure to serve either the place or their own community in it. I am forced, against all my hopes and inclinations, to regard the history of my people here as the progress of the doom of what I value most in the world: the life and health of the earth, the peacefulness of human communities and households.
>
> And so here, in the place I love more than any other . . . , I am more painfully divided within myself than I could be in any other place.[2]

In the mid-1990s, when I was a teenager (a few years after skiing down the prairie cow pasture hills lost its appeal), I spent a part of each summer with a church group that journeyed out to the Pine

Ridge Indian Reservation, a seven-hour drive from home. It was your fairly typical youth service trip: We spent mornings facilitating a day camp with local children and afternoons doing work projects and hauling supplies around to various locations. We taught the kids sing-along songs, and the cook at the center that we used as a home base taught us how to say a few table prayers in the Lakota language. In addition to playing games, sharing meals, and making crafts with the youth, some days we drove them back to their homes in our big white church van. Pine Ridge is in Oglala Lakota County (known as Shannon County until 2014), one of the areas in the United States with the lowest per capita income, and this fact was glaringly apparent to my fourteen-year-old self as we dropped off the kids where they lived. One day when driving through one of the neighborhoods in Pine Ridge proper, I remember feeling awash with guilt, incredulity that I had so much when so many were born into so little. South Dakota doesn't have mild winters, especially not on the western prairie, where Pine Ridge is located. So many people were without adequate housing.

That afternoon, I felt disgusted that we—rich, mostly white Americans—were invading the personal space of people whom our forefathers had stolen from and oppressed. The story I was living, the one that was supporting me so well, was also a story that was failing another group of people. My teenage mind didn't really know what to do with these thoughts, but looking back now, I can identify that trip, and, more specifically, that drive around the local neighborhood, as the experience that made me start to question what was really going on in the world. The issues, such as alcoholism or poverty on reservations, that the mainstream media tends to highlight are systemic—they have arisen due to years of genocide, cultural erasure, and white supremacy. There are reasons, and lots of them, why things are the way they are. The herds of bison that historically sustained the Lakota people were nearly wiped out due to habitat loss and settler hunting initiatives (that were designed to destroy this essential source of food and materials, with the goal of starving Indigenous people into submission). The land where Pine Ridge sits is dry and largely ill-suited for farming, so government nutrition programs and convenience stores often stand in as a poor substitute. (However, farming *is* done successfully by some organizations that are presently leading the regenerative agriculture movement in the Pine Ridge community, including Thunder Valley Community Development Corporation.[3])

There is also a lot that folks not actively involved in Native American communities simply don't see or hear about—or consider the origins of. Mission trips themselves are a direct product of colonization—something that makes me deeply uncomfortable[4] to acknowledge, but something that's irrefutably true, as much as it is complicated and nuanced in the myriad ways individuals and communities interact with one another. Overall, though, when we well-meaning white folks swoop in to "fix" things, *we* are the group that's ultimately benefiting. We may have done some helpful acts of service during our stay and changed some things as a result of our immersion in the community, but the trip centered on our white experience. Even now, I have to continually check myself to see where my motivation to help is coming from: guilt or genuine empathy. Sometimes it's hard to discern.

When I was growing up, issues such as America's history of slavery and the fact that our town was built on colonized land weren't things that anybody talked about much. Those summers in Pine Ridge opened my eyes, and my eleventh-grade English teacher was instrumental in continuing my education about privilege, inequality, and the need for racial justice to pursue peace. He assigned books by Native American and Black authors. We watched raw footage from concentration camps during the Holocaust. We had discussions about the Wounded Knee Massacre on Pine Ridge (as well as what is often referred to as the occupation at Wounded Knee that occurred in 1973). We dug pretty deep for a small-town midwestern junior English class into some of what history books often leave out or gloss over. Literature has a way of shedding light on important dark (often deliberately made more palatable) places in the history of a people. That year in English class, I gained a sense of what was truly going on in the world. I caught a glimpse of the dark underbelly of the beast. While going through old boxes of stuff after moving into my current home, I found some slightly yellowed papers and projects from that class, and they radiated anger and guilt and confusion alongside a developing love of the earth and awareness of a harsh reality. Those formative years uncovered a new path and opened a door that can't be closed.

When I asked my friend Juliana, who identifies as Chicana, about how connected she feels to her familial history, she said, "I'm a fifth-generation Colorado native with Ute and Dine ancestry, but I don't have the public records to document my past. It's all been washed away by weather, sun, rain, and gentrification." She said she feels very connected to her roots now but that she didn't always feel that way. Decades ago, she'd felt brown on the outside and white on the inside. She went on to explain that her cousins grew up in southern Colorado but in an area where a large population of Chicanos migrated from northern New Mexico. Her grandparents migrated to southern Colorado canyon country, and Juliana was raised in a county famous for Klan activity. As a result, the Black community had been scared off or lynched, and the laborers became the "brown-skinned children of the sun, the Mexicanos." Her parents were punished in public school for speaking Spanish. Their names were anglicized. Julian became Jack, and Eloisa became Louise. When I asked her what was hard about digging into her origin, she said the "hard digs" included discovering that her ancestors were Indigenous slaves to Spaniards, Mexicans, and religious white men looking for converts—that her ancestors were dehumanized.

Sorting through the complex questions raised by differences in race, class, and privilege will be the work of my lifetime. My ancestral homelands in Europe haven't been overtaken by a dominant migrant group, and my great-great-grandparents came to America of their own free will. I have never lived in a black- or brown-skinned body in a world that caters to whiteness. I can only imagine what it is like, and that's not even close to the same thing. As my friend and writing colleague Ellie Roscher has said, "Whiteness is a character in my books." It's the lens through which I view the world. I have traveled and had extended stays in more diverse areas, but my everyday experiences reinforce the fact that I can choose to think about race or not. People of color (people who are, in fact, the global majority) don't get that choice.

In 2016, Indigenous peoples from all over the world gathered in North Dakota to stop the Dakota Access Pipeline, a project that destroyed sacred sites and continues to threaten the water source of millions. Police in riot gear made arrests, and peaceful protesters were injured. Some argued that the police were just doing their jobs and following orders. Some members of law enforcement laid down their badges, but most did not; they had families for which to provide, or they believed they were on the side that was doing the right thing. In North Dakota, the state of the Bakken oil fields—fields that, when fully lit, can be seen from space—pipelines mean money, and money often means people do whatever it takes to get what feels like enough.

Elders and youth and members of the press were charged with felonies and trespassing on lands where their ancestors are buried. Horses and people were shot with rubber bullets. The cycle of violence continued, and continues still, even though we know what we know. Indigenous Nations have been oppressed for hundreds of years all over this continent. Big oil and excessive energy consumption continue to pillage the earth, leaving scars and destruction that disproportionately hurts folks who don't get the benefits of all that electricity and cheap gas. The prairie has seen much pain and destruction due to the colonization that took place (and continues to this day). This heartland of America may seem like it's flyover country, but the knowledge in these grasslands and rolling hills is deep and wise. The Great Plains, like so many geological regions, have absorbed the blood and tears of generations—this land is not a stranger to pain. Nor is it a stranger to the beauty that rises despite destruction.

When reflecting on her origin, Juliana spoke of her connection to nature and described it as her "roots to place" in the world. Years ago, she made a pilgrimage from her home to where her father migrated from a New Mexico village on the Pecos River, to a village on the Arkansas River in southern Colorado. She said the sky, the river, the soil, the rock formations, the birds, the vegetation, and the animals became characters in her poetry.[5] She writes about these locations where *mi gente*—her ancestors—are buried, where they were sheepherders and farmers until the water rights were sold or stolen and they had to migrate north.

Hannah, one of my wellness coaching colleagues, believes that uncovering and connecting to our roots, our origin, is an ever-evolving process. She believes that "the roots have always been there, solidly planted in the ground, protected from the harshness of the world." Her father is Anishinaabe from the Hiawatha First Nation, and her mother immigrated from France not long after World War II. Hannah spent summers on the reservation or in France as she was growing up. Because the cultures on each side of her family are so different, it was really hard to find the balance between them. Sometimes it felt like there was a war going on for her identity. When she went to college, she truly began her journey to feel fully connected to herself. For Hannah, little decisions to claim her dual identity happen each day. She makes Niish artwork and jewelry. She immerses herself in content from her nations. She calls her relatives. She speaks French and sings to her son in Ojibwemowin. She smudges, prays, and thanks the Creator. She advocates and educates. She told me that every time she does any of these things, she is creating harmony with her origin.

Sometimes I wonder what sorts of ceremonies and rituals my long-ago ancestors, the people who were indigenous to a landmass somewhere in what is now Europe, might have performed. Did they dance to celebrate the earth and give thanks and connect to their spiritual center? Would I feel something if I were to attend one of those ancient ceremonies now? I wonder what their connection to the natural world was like all those years ago, and what aspects of it got to me, all these generations later. My ancestors were indigenous to a region of the earth long ago, though the relatives that I can identify in my family history played a role in colonization. I can't change that, but I can take action to right inherited wrongs, and I can learn more about Norse mythology and the earth-based spiritualities of ancient Germanic peoples. I can keep my eyes open to the patterns that keep repeating in history and further develop my own relationship with the energy I sense in the land. I grew up on the prairie, yet there's a part of me that's always been drawn to the forest and to large bodies of water: Walking into the cool shelter of tall trees always feels like getting a little piece of myself back. Communing with the deep blue depths of Lake Superior is grounding in a different way than being among a sea of tall grass but just as essential. I wonder if that's the generational imprint of the old country, of the fjords of Norway or the Baltic Sea, that still lingers in my bones.

As I was finishing this chapter, a new year started, a time when I always reflect on these words of Kent Nerburn: "You must look closely in this dark month. Examine the backs of your hands and the movements of your fingers. Place your thumbprints on the edges of old bowls. Immerse yourself in ceremonies of the ordinary. Do not seek large issues. In January one needs ritual, not philosophy."[6]

In January, I'm lighting fires again in the woodstove each day, a ritual reclaimed in adulthood after growing up in a house heated only with wood. It feels good to resume this daily practice, the one that connects me to those who came before, who lit hearth fires decades and centuries past, even in far-off lands across the sea. This ritual (that's also a bit of a chore) of hauling logs, splitting them into kindling, clearing the old ashes, stacking up that kindling just so, and introducing flame to paper "marries the mundane to the sacred."[7]

What if we took Mr. Nerburn's advice and placed our attention on things like the edges of old bowls and the backs of our hands? I can choose to contemplate the delicate heaviness of a pottery mug, the way my fingers fit around its curves as I step into the wintry air to see how the steam rises when the temperature is colder than comfortable. What of our origin might come to light in the lines on our faces as we brush our teeth or the cracks in old bowls as we wash them by hand? What can be uncovered by peering deeply into the ordinary actions of our days and discovering the rituals that already exist inside them? I can create my own ceremony and piece it together as I continue to uncover my own truth.

There is power in ceremonies of the ordinary—power that isn't flashy or quick moving or even nice to look at sometimes. But it could just be the antidote we need to continue doing the work necessary to move forward. Reflecting on where we come from isn't easy. Following the trail to where we originate often leads to more questions than answers. Digging into family history can uncover unhealed wounds, from generational trauma to forgotten or buried secrets. For some who were adopted, or those whose ancestors were born into slavery, or those who simply don't know who their parents were for whatever reason—from being displaced by war as an infant to dissociating to survive torture—it can be a long time before answers are found. Sometimes it's not possible to find the answers that are sought. Digging for the truth often includes a more mountainous, steeper climb than we feel ready for. The dust that gets churned up as we excavate doesn't always settle where we'd like it to. But the time to go there is now. The weary world wants to rejoice, and the only way we'll get to that place together is if we dig for the truth, starting with ourselves.

Listening to the Land

What's the true story of the land you're on, and how does it influence your choices?

These days, I make my home in Minnesota, the land of ten thousand lakes. Though I wasn't born here, I now live in what's known as *America's Little Sweden*. Incorporated in 1894, Lindström is one of the small towns in the area. It was settled by a man named Daniel Lindström—he left his homeland of Sweden for the prospect of a new start on American soil in 1853. The water tower is an enormous coffee pot, Dala horses abound, and the Swedish flag is flown with pride. People know how to make *lefse*, drink *glögg*, and some even enjoy eating *lutefisk*. Lindstrom has a sister city in Sweden: Tingsryd. (A few of the other small towns close by have sister cities as well.) There's a wilderness park within the city limits called Allemansrätt, which in Swedish essentially means "everyone's right"—a concept that takes the view that all people should be able to freely access wilderness and reap the benefits that come from doing so regularly, as long as it is done with respect for the land and others. You can almost feel the commitment to heritage and the deep bond that gets passed on through families in the air around here, which in modern culture is so often lost. The ancestors of many in this community that's built around a chain of lakes were neighbors to my Norwegian great-great-grandparents in Scandinavia. I appreciate the sense of belonging to a place that keeps this community's Nordic roots nourished.

The community in which I live is steeped in tradition—origin is important to many people here. There are multiple public displays of Scandinavian and agricultural history in the area. The Gammelgården Museum[1] is the only open-air museum in the United States devoted to preserving, presenting, and promoting Swedish immigrant heritage, and it's a fifteen-minute drive from my house. People here are proud of where they came from and of the generations that have made a life in this area. It's fun to go to the museum for Midsommar Dag (Midsummer Day) in June or the Spelmansstämma (an "outdoor gathering of fiddlers" in Swedish) in August to listen to fiddle music and celebrate the Swedish heritage that was brought here from the old country. The Karl Oskar House,[2] another local landmark, commemorates what life was like for the newly transplanted immigrants in the late 1800s. I can feel a sense of connection when I visit or attend events at each place. Many Scandinavians settled here because the lakes, forests, and valleys reminded them of the homeland they left behind. And though the connection feels like a loose one, it reminds me that celebrating one's cultural heritage is important.

Katie Malchow, the executive director of the Chisago Lakes Visitors Bureau, said in an interview with local news station Kare11,

"We very much celebrate the fact that we have that Swedish heritage." She also mentioned that "the thing that gets a little overlooked is the fact that this area was occupied early on by Native Americans." I find myself wondering about the people, the Dakota and Ojibwe, who were here well before the Swedes made their way to this river valley and chain of lakes and what their living descendants think about what gets celebrated in the area now.

During the days that lead up to the summer solstice, I like to start the days with a trail run on the bluffs of the St. Croix River, followed by time in the newly planted garden, a meal of fresh asparagus or greens with lemon thyme, and a leisurely evening stroll amid the quickly growing seedlings. In late spring, mosquitoes have yet to hatch in full force, there are still no deer flies, and the loons have just returned to the lake, sending their haunting cries out into the night as the full moon rises. You can almost hear the reflection that the brightness of the moon shines on the lake as the energy of the earth moves through another cycle and shifts into a higher gear.

About ten miles from my house, just across the St. Croix River,[3] also the border with Wisconsin, there's a place called Standing Cedars Community Land Conservancy. Fifteen hundred acres in total, it's been set aside for preservation. There are a few marked trails and some signs of the ski hill that used to operate there in the 1950s, but mostly it's just acres of wilderness that are being allowed to do what they will do.

Philadelphia Community Farm (PCF) sits adjacent to Standing Cedars and also stewards a section of the conservancy. One of the first Community Supported Agriculture (CSA) programs in the Midwest, it was established in 1989 as a nonprofit. Through

Buttermilk Falls Folk School, they welcome school and civic groups of all ages, and the resident community carries on the tradition of intergenerational, multi-abled shared living. They steward and tend the land and responsibly use it for nature-centered education programs and retreats. Biodynamic regenerative agriculture and social justice remain their highest priorities. I have facilitated many retreats on the property, and each time participants mention how powerful it is to walk the area and engage in the practices that make up the backbone of this intentional community.

The first time I visited the natural spring that feeds Buttermilk Falls, the waterfall on the property, I was guided there by PCF's executive director at the time, Christina Beck. She had lived on the land for many years and was in charge of cultivating community and ensuring things run smoothly, from finances to programming to relationships. We'd gathered together with five other female-identifying folks, diverse in age, cultural background, and vocation, to celebrate the season with ritual, be present for one another in compassionate listening, and mindfully spend time with the land. Christina led the group to the spring, which she loves for its subterranean cool, equisetum, ferns, and watercress. Gathered around the alcove where the water bubbles up from the ground, we took turns filling a vessel, gave thanks for the waters, and drank. Most of the people there I'd never met and didn't have much in common with by way of day-to-day lived experience, but we came together by actively practicing gratitude for the life-giving waters of the land.

At PCF, they are actively shifting how they operate to reflect the "condemnation of structural racism and systemic oppression." In a solidarity statement written in June of 2020, they state, "We believe that everyone is deserving of a relationship with nature that can aid in mutual restoration of the spirit. To that end, we work in regenerative agriculture to share food grown on this land with those impacted by the uprising and through our mutual aid CSA shares program, devote resources to exploring the history of this land, reparations to Indigenous Nations, and practice caring for the land and each other with dignity and a clear sense of interdependence."[4]

One section of Standing Cedars (that you walk through when taking the hiking trail that loops from the main animal barn at PCF) is known as Buffalo Skull. Some people I've talked to in the community have said that Buffalo Skull, located on a bluff high above the St. Croix River, is the site of some ancient Indigenous mounds. Before settlers came to the area, this land was inhabited by eastern bands of Dakota and, later, as fur trading in the 1700s continued west, Ojibwe people. The Dakota and Ojibwe coexisted quite peacefully for a long time, but a war between the two groups eventually pushed the Dakota further west, leaving the Ojibwe in control of the upper St. Croix River Valley. A series of treaties between 1825 and 1854 ceded these lands (among many other pieces of wilderness) to the federal government. The Homestead Act of 1862 capped off the conversion of over five million acres of once tribal lands to settlers, leaving the Indigenous Nations with much smaller areas of reservation land (which was a poor substitute for the vast tracts of wilderness that had supported their way of life for generations).

According to the Minnesota Office of the State Archaeologist, the landscape of this region is "dotted with earthworks or mounds built by Native American peoples before the arrival of Euro-American settlers. Such earthworks are frequently located along bluffs and

terraces which overlook rivers."⁵ The folks in the community who
are familiar with the history of the Standing Cedars and PCF whom
I've talked to don't think any mounds at Standing Cedars were used
for burial, though some Indigenous mounds around the region were.
Another community member told me she'd heard the area was a
peaceful gathering place for various Indigenous groups due to the
abundance of natural springs. Whatever has happened on this piece
of earth over the years, as you walk the land now, there's a sense of
something else, something old, something sacred, something that
is a little outside of my grasp, riding on the breeze that ruffles hair
left loose. Oak trees and tall grasses sway in the late spring air, and
something in my collective human consciousness knows that land,
somewhere, is part of my origin, and I am part of the land. I'm part
of the land where I walk but also part of a land I may never touch
with my body. People forced to flee their homelands due to war or
environmental disaster or sea-level rise are part of a land they may
never touch again, yet they have a right to connect to the land that
becomes their new foundation. The story of human relationship
with land can be a complicated and complex one.

When I asked Chrystal Odin, CSA administrator and board
officer at PCF, what she hears when she listens to the land where the
farm rests, she said it's the trees that speak to her the most, that they
feel undervalued and in need of honoring, especially the maples. She
also said the land speaks of periods of overexpectation and neglect.
Part of her work as a biodynamic gardener is establishing practices
that replenish the soil. She also prioritizes making promises to the
trees on behalf of human beings. Her connection to the land and
the plant spirits are the basis of her vocation as a vegetable grower.

Without this connection, she said she would not be able to serve the earth in a healing way or be given the opportunity to heal herself. She also spoke of the importance of honoring the animal life that's present where one lives. On every piece of land she has worked, a different species of animal has made itself most seen as the baseline energy. At the last farm she and her family called home, there were many tree frogs and salamanders: she came in contact with at least six a day. At PCF, it is snakes, lizards, and skinks that she sees almost daily. Noticing the animal energy at the land where she lives drives her call to reconnect with Source and the sacred circle that connects all of life on earth.

As the full moon rises in late spring, birds of all sorts are eager to continue filling the air with their songs, and frogs chirp and chuckle at all hours of the day. Snakes sun themselves on warming rocks. The forest floor is a dense carpet of vibrantly green foliage after months of brown and white dormancy. It's a time of planting seeds, of nourishment, of newness, and of growth. It's a time of shockingly bright grass and apple trees that like to flaunt their pink blossoms. It's the return of dirt under fingernails, the feel of soil between toes, and feet that never quite get clean. The icy and muddy part of spring is done, and life is in full swing. I can almost feel myself remembering what it is like to be a part of the earth. If I pay attention, I can sense what parts of myself want to emerge right alongside everything else.

Christina told me that it's the layers of her own ancestors who were farmers, and future descendants, who compel her to make every effort toward being in right relationship with the land and its protectors. She said these layers contain whispers of the people who dwelled on the land prior to the European American settlers. She has consciously cultivated her connection to nature as a way to balance her intensive work in the human realm. This connection to earth makes her soul feel alive and awake. From this place, she can actively work informed by nature's wisdom.

Fifteen hundred miles southeast of PCF is Flagler Beach in Florida, where my colleague Rowan makes her current home. When I asked her what happens when she listens to the story of the history of the land where she lives, she told me she practices listening to the wind that blows in from the sea, carrying with it salty air and the scent of birth. Her home is on the ancestral lands of the Timucua people, and prior to that, the Paleoindians, who left artifacts dating back thirteen to twenty thousand years. She's surrounded by mineral freshwater springs, salt- and freshwater estuaries, and the great Atlantic Ocean. She says when she listens, "I hear the stories of survival. I hear the stories of connection with animals, plants, and nature relationships. I hear suffering at the hands of colonists, and I hear the stories, drumbeats, and songs of survival and hope." Like Chrystal at PCF, Rowan mentioned the importance of listening to the nonhuman forms of life. "The plants speak lessons of respect, for myself and for others. And then the animals . . . the wild boar, the poisonous snakes and spiders, the incessant biting things, the soaring wood storks, pink spoonbills, hard-shelled crabs, alligators, armadillos, the miraculous sea turtles making their way to the sea. Living creatures surround me and remind me to breathe, to listen to their lessons, and to notice them all." Rowan has noticed that all of these forms of life are armed with their own unique tools of fight, flight, or freeze. They're fully protected by armor, shells, or venom. She's noticed that the lessons of resilience and perseverance tend to rise up from the wild ones.

Sometimes, like Christina, Chrystal, and Rowan, I can hear the whispers of the people who were here long before those of us who walk this land now and the hum of the creature and plant life that abounds. As I run the wooded trails of Standing Cedars high on the river bluff, it's as if my own breathing mixes with the breath of those who walked or ran on this land generations ago. I sense my animal kin breathing alongside me. I can hear the story of the land humming. I can feel the call to reconciliation and the need for reparations. I can sense the part of me that originates in Gaia, Mother Earth, herself.

As I continued to reflect on Swedish and Native American heritage, I became acquainted with another Christina through a parent group we're both a part of. She's a fellow mom of school-age kids in the Chisago Lakes area. Instead of just continuing to wonder what contemporary Indigenous folks might think about what gets celebrated in my community these days, I asked. Christina Ettestad grew up attending and competing in powwows with her Mdewakanton Dakota relatives. When I asked her what she thought about the Swedish heritage focus in our shared community, she said, "I think it's great to recognize the foundation on which this community was built. It's interesting to learn about the Swedish ties our community has and those who helped to establish its presence today. I don't think it takes away from our Native heritage to recognize the ties our community has with another country. As a Native American woman, I find it important to also embrace and celebrate the ties with the area's original inhabitants. It's part of our history." Christina reminded me that "for those who have questions, the only way to learn is to ask." We have to ask the questions, and we have to listen to the response, which can be full of nuance and difference, depending on an individual's unique perspective.

There's another place called Ki Chi Saga Park, just two miles from my house, where I like to go to trail run. In Ojibwe, *ki chi saga* means "fair and lovely waters." This park is where the Karl Oskar House sits, the humble farmhouse mentioned earlier that's filled with period pieces and information about the Swedes who came here in the late 1800s. In a way, it's a celebration of a current community's history keeping company with the whispers of those who were here first.

When we open to the true story of the land, there is no going back to pretending we didn't hear what the land tells us when we truly listen. We can start to connect our own story to that of the land we're on and ensure we are taking strides to decolonize our actions, honor the land's energy, and add the healing necessary for our collective thriving.

Claiming Who You Are

What would it take to truly claim who you are?

After digging into the truth and listening to the land, it's time to claim who you are. One way to do that is through story—setting aside the false and claiming the true. Barry Lopez wrote, in his book *Crow and Weasel*,[1] "Remember this one thing, said Badger. The stories people tell have a way of taking care of them. If stories come to you, care for them. And learn to give them away where they are needed. Sometimes a person needs a [true] story more than food to stay alive."

Stories aren't always easy to tell, and it can be really hard to listen to the true ones. Life on earth is messy and raw and always evolving. The stories we share keep us going. They help us see each other.

Think of a story you tell yourself—perhaps a story the media tells that you've internalized, perhaps a story you've been acting out to appease a family member, perhaps a story you hear over and over again about how a person with your background is supposed to be—any story that part of you knows just isn't fully true.

After you've identified the story, take a moment to pause. What message are you getting? Then reflect on whose message it really is: Who benefits from your acceptance of it?

What's really true?

"Speak up. I can't hear you."

"Aren't you going to smile?"

"Oh, you must be shy."

As a child, I did this thing my parents called "swallowing my smile."

When someone I didn't know looked at me, spoke to me, or tried to get me to interact with them, I'd look down and bite my lips. It was my way of coping with social anxiety.

Looking down and biting my lips seemed safe. Engaging with strangers, even well-meaning ones, was scary. What if I said the wrong thing or, worse, couldn't think of anything to say at all? What if I blushed? What if the other person thought I was strange? What if I had to repeat myself in order to be understood and then couldn't remember what I said the first time?

At an early age, I came to the conclusion that being a quiet person wasn't something to be proud of—that it was something I needed to "work on" or "overcome" to be a successful human being. I thought that being quiet was a defect, a quality that weakened my value as a person.

Consider the need to earn participation points in school: I never got those. I don't think I ever raised my hand in class, even if I knew the answer. And the teachers who liked to call on students at random? Those class periods were the absolute worst—I'd leave a sweaty mess after waiting in fear all period to be called on while composing possible answers to questions in my head just in case. If I was called on, I always—always—turned a bright shade of pink. I hated that about myself so much.

Then I met Miss Binnie. She was my sixth-grade English teacher. At age twenty-five, she had a full head of prematurely gray hair, and she always wore colorful scarves. She exuded the confidence and ease that always seemed to elude me. I wanted to be her.

One day after class, she told me that being a quiet person was okay, and, in fact, being quiet was a good thing—that it meant that I was thoughtful and attentive. She told me that she got nervous talking in front of the class sometimes, that I didn't have to try to be louder, and that blushing was a very normal thing. I don't remember any of my other sixth-grade teachers, but I remember her.

Dominant culture often feels like a world that caters to the extrovert, to the one who shouts the loudest. Outgoing and loud over reserved and quiet in a duel. It can be tempting to think of those who are quiet or soft-spoken as weaker than those who are loud and abrasive. The description of "good leader" is often in step with "charismatic extrovert." I used to try and try and try to be louder and less reserved. For a great many years, I thought that to be loud and outgoing meant to be good enough to be liked. I didn't want to always be labeled as the quiet one, the one who wouldn't respond when too nervous or who said "pass" when it was her turn to talk.

When I was in the seventh grade, I can clearly recall mustering up all of my courage and energy to engage in a conversation with one of the popular girls. She said, "Oh, you're kind of cool when you talk." I remember being elated, followed by wondering how I was going to talk enough to maintain my newfound coolness. I gained another layer of appreciation for the companionship of the prairie grass in the field near my house. It didn't care if I talked or not.

In the professional realm, it's been easy to get sucked into thinking that to verbally contribute in every meeting is the only way to make sure I'm seen as a good employee. A manager I had once, years ago, pulled me aside a few weeks into a new job and asked if attending meetings where everyone was required to contribute verbally was too much for me to handle. In retrospect, it was a kind gesture, but at the time all I felt was shame.

I can't pinpoint when exactly I came to the realization that gregarious doesn't actually mean better or when I settled in the place of acceptance that I'm never going to be a loud person who enjoys being up front (and that trying to be isn't going to help anybody). There are, of course, still times when I wish I interacted with the world differently, that speaking up and out came easier to me. As a writer who has to get up in front of crowds on occasion to read from my work or answer questions or even give a prepared talk, I still blush, stumble over my words, or forget the brilliant speech I'd given in my head countless times. If I'm being truly honest, even calling in a food order is nerve racking. But gradually, I have come to claim my quietness and have figured out how to navigate through the times when engaging in life verbally is just something that I have to do. It's gotten easier with age, but I doubt it'll ever come naturally. In doing so, I have uncovered a bit more of the joy that can be present in life—the sort of joy that only shows up when I own my character-istics rather than being ashamed of them.

Claiming my quietness has allowed me to show up authentically in my days. It's helped me put my energy where it can do the most good. It allows me the space to watch the steam rising from a hot cup of tea and the space to savor the first sip. It's helped me ensure that I spend my first and last moments of the day engaged in things that are truly life-giving. It's helped me find the modes of communication that are most effective. Appreciating my traits helps me notice the crunch of snow underfoot and the tiny tracks left by my nonhuman neighbors. It is in the love I give and the love I accept, the bound-aries I set and the boundaries I honor, the values I live by and the willingness to peer, even if just for a little while, at something from someone else's perspective. No one walks through life in exactly the same way, and that's what makes claiming your own way of doing so so important.

Quinn Gathercole, in an essay published in *The Wayfarer Maga-zine*, writes about the internal struggle that happened as they moved toward and fully claimed their nonbinary identity. Quinn opens the essay by telling the story of the first time they tried out a new name by telling it to the barista at a coffee shop and the fear that came with it of being found out as a fraud. Quinn writes, after hearing the name they were trying on called out for the order, "That was the day I ceased being someone society had decided was a woman. That day I embraced who I really felt I was on the inside and I never looked back."[2] Quinn compares gender to planets and sees themself as something altogether separate from male or female; Quinn says if men and women are from Mars and Venus, well, nonbinary folks are from Saturn. Being able to own their identity as a nonbinary person has allowed them to be more fully who they are.

In Catherine Gildiner's groundbreaking book about five of her most heroic therapy patients, *Good Morning, Monster*,[3] she shares the story of Danny, a man who came to therapy unable to grieve the loss of his wife and young daughter after they died in a car crash. Over a period of several years, he shares and processes the horrific abuse (mental, physical, and sexual) he endured while enrolled at an Indian residential school, as well as the deep pain due to being taken from his parents and their hunting/trapping way of life as a young boy. Eventually he was able to come to a place where he could move forward through the grief, fully himself, and he did that by claiming his story as well as his Indigenous heritage. The deep trauma of residential schools in the United States and Canada continues to be uncovered, and while it's not a chapter that's easy to read, it's a chapter that's true. Truth, even painful truth, must be acknowledged so that new chapters can be written.

So many people have stories that are incredibly hard to share or that are difficult to access from the depths of unconscious memory. (These are best excavated and worked through with the support of a therapist or other trusted person or group.) Trauma is woven into many chapters for many different groups of people and individuals.

It can take a great deal of courage to fully claim the identity that is ours. Doing so can be a risk, a painful or even dangerous one, in a society that doesn't widely accept certain ways of being and where many stories have been hidden or minimized.

As I wrote in a poetry collection called *Cold Spring Hallelujah*, "Claiming is not an easy task, just like telling a true story can be the most challenging feat of a lifetime. But acknowledging and giving voice to the story that wants to be claimed is the first step—something that has to happen to shore up the foundation for a beautiful way of being in the world."[4]

I have to continually remind myself that the world needs more quiet leadership. More listening. Less shouting and trying to be the one who gets the attention. Less trying to be something I am not just because dominant culture says a certain way of being is desirable. I've been described as quiet, introverted, and the dreaded *shy* more times than I can count, and it's okay to be those things. My voice is needed, and so is yours, no matter its volume. Our voices can be heard in ways that come through without trying to be something we aren't.

You can make a positive difference in the world by being who you already are. Claiming who you are helps you do this.

No matter what ways of being fit your person, when it feels right to push yourself outside of that much-discussed comfort zone, do it. There's room to grow and do hard things. But there's also room to own what makes you who you are and to lean into the ways of being that suit you best. For me, that means claiming that being quiet and soft-spoken is part of who I am. It means letting go of trying to be louder. As a white, cisgender, straight person, it also means continually discerning when I really do need to push myself to speak up and when it's not my voice that's needed. We all have different qualities that require claiming, but claim them we must. We need to use our strength in ways that work best. Because when we do, we're stronger for it, and the story of the world gets better.

It's not easy to do, but there is such power in considering what's ours and claiming the truth—the truth that says we're worthy of well-being and belonging. This requires slowing down, listening, and practicing self-compassion. It can be a hard road, and those inner negativity gremlins can be tough to shake. Old stories can leave marks from years of repetition. The stories we tell ourselves in our own minds shape how we operate in the world. It's important to continually seek the balance of telling our own, claiming our truth, and listening to those truths of others. Stories are the heartbeat of humanity, the way we make sense of the world and ourselves.

Claiming your story—who you truly are—is worth it. It prepares you for the journey.

An Invitation to Tap into Your Roots

What if you could accept this wild dare?

Claim your roots, your connection to creation.

Nestle into ways of being that allow you to live well while letting the rivers and lakes and clouds of dreams invite you to take that step into the unknown.

Go deep with your gratitude when the sun pierces your view. As the fog lifts, let the call of a crane remind you to look up from the old worn path that everyone else decided to take.

See grace wherever your eyes land. Notice, and claim, every opportunity to practice compassion for all living things.

Let go of expectation and ride the torrents of change to a place of peace and healing.

Rest on the stump of an old evergreen and feel the passing of the times. Mourn what is gone and dying and celebrate the beauty that can still be found in the lichen that grow at the graves of the clear-cut forests and the tears that run down the ruined mountaintops. Remember that all is not lost.

Be who you are called to be—mind, body, and spirit—in full wildness and wholly grounded in truth.

Be the love.

Send your howls to the wind and bear witness.

Accept the invitation to acknowledge your roots and claim your place as part of the earth's body.

Listen to the stories that need to be heard.

Dare to pay attention and tell about it.

Part Two

Journey

jour·ney
ˈjərnē/
an act of traveling from one place to another

As the saying goes, a journey of a thousand miles begins with a single step. Indeed it does. Likewise, every step is a journey in and of itself. There is no arriving—there is only the journey and being present for it. That journey can take us far from home or deep into our inner lives, but no matter what direction we go, our journey leaves the marks that make us who we are and reminds us that, as Jacobus Johannes Leeuw wrote, "The mystery of life is not a problem to be solved; it is a reality to be experienced."[1] The journey leads us back to ourselves if we pay attention to where we're headed.

Charting a Course

How does exploring what's under your desire help you chart a course forward, even if you feel lost some of the time?

I'm in a dusty red four-speed 1992 Toyota that doesn't have air-conditioning, driving west on I-90 across South Dakota with the windows wide open, on my way to Colorado. It's August, and a cassette tape is playing since no radio stations will tune in without static. After acres of cornfields turn into miles of grassy pasture, after the Missouri River Valley gives way to rolling plains, after I see a sign for Buffalo Gap National Grassland and cross through the barren beauty of Badlands spires reaching toward the sky, after the signs for Wall Drug that say, "Wait, you missed it!" After all of that, I finally come to the place where the Black Hills loom in the distance, and I marvel at the sudden change in the horizon.

There is a reason these mountains are called what they are—when they appear in the windshield, it is like looking into layer upon layer of an artist's delicate coal shading against the brightness of a late-summer sky. I am astonished at the majestic expanse that commands my attention and the welcoming darkness of what lies ahead. Surely there is myth and magic to be found once I arrive at this oasis. This land is known as Paha Sapa in Lakota language, and I can see why the Lakota people hold this land as sacred.

And then at some point (that I never quite notice as it happens) as I continue on the westward journey, it's gone. Once I reach the point where identifying individual hills and trees is possible, the black has vanished, and only the landscape remains. They are just hills, now—beautiful and sacred as they always were, but the mystery that came with the space that was once between me and the place I sought is as gone as the distance that was closed to nothing. When I look up and out past the place where the hills give way to grasslands again, I can see hints of the next place that I seek and the color that tints that desire to arrive. The myth and magic remain just around the next corner.

Every day we interact with others who are longing for something. I might be so bold as to say that everyone reading these words longs for something too, whether that something feels completely unattainable or is as easy as walking down the hall for a cup of afternoon coffee. The things we want, the benefits that we hope to see come from our efforts in living a fulfilling life, the vision of success that we are working toward—it's so easy to get caught up in the outcome. I tend to get drawn into the thinking of "making it" or "being successful with attaining the goal" or "measuring notable progress." I doubt I'm alone.

That makes me wonder what it would look like to just *be* with desire—to bear witness to it, to inhabit it fully, to not wish it away.

There is something profound in truly feeling what we feel without trying to change it—in being right where we are right now, regardless of the external circumstances or the progress that could potentially still be made. I wonder what it would look like to just sit with a feeling, be it longing, pain, irritation, or just the urge to compose three emails at once, and let that feeling do its work in us, even if it's uncomfortable or makes us look at something in life that we'd rather not look at. Maybe we would feel less stuck all the time. Maybe we could then see the beauty in the shadowy distant hills and let it carry us into whatever horizon might invite us in next. Maybe we would find that the myth and magic are always within grasp, waiting for us to notice them.

Being with desire, well, that can mean a lot of things, but one of them is rooting down into the present, letting that connection be enough to provide a foundation for whatever is next on the horizon. We don't always know where we'll be headed next when we're charting a course, however. Sometimes we get lost.

Being lost is quite an experience, to put it mildly. More accurately, being lost has the potential to be disorienting, disconcerting, scary, anxiety-inducing, exhilarating, dangerous, or liberating.

I did eventually make it to my Colorado destination in that dusty four-speed Toyota. And on a day hike in the Maroon Bells Wilderness, my hiking companions and I lost the trail.

We'd set out early in the morning with a topographic map of the area, along with daypacks full of snacks, water, and rain gear. We were on the Marble side of the wilderness area, not the more populated Aspen side, and the route we picked that day was not well used (or maintained) that summer, especially as we gained altitude and reached the tree line. Just before midday, a storm started moving in as we picked our way over an ominously darkening snow- and ice-covered pass. As we started to make a speedy descent back toward the promise of tree cover, we realized our trail had faded to nothing, and there were no rock cairns in sight—in our haste, we had veered off course. We had a general idea of where we were, but the official, marked way to move down the mountain was uncertain. We were disoriented, and we had to make choices based on our reality at the time.

In the time leading up to stepping back onto a well-worn trail, I suppose we were officially lost. We didn't know exactly where to go next, but in those moments of unknowing, I noticed more details. I noticed how the wind shifted in the trees, how the mountain seemed to breathe in and out as the storm rumbled overhead, how the delicate green water plants in the stream we followed in lieu of the trail shimmered under the weight of tiny water droplets. I felt the life of the mountain flowing through me as the sense of being fully present was intensified with the uncertainty of our path.

Mary Oliver wrote, "Sometimes the desire to be lost again, as long ago, comes over me like a vapor."[1]

She's talking about a time when she was a child and she walked upstream, away from her parents. They thought she was lost, and maybe she truly was for a time. But in that experience, what stuck to her soul was simply a sense of the happiness that comes from feeling cool water push against bare skin, noticing a delicate shade of green, allowing for a heart opening. A sense of being pulled toward what truly matters.

I think that's what sticks to me too—or at least that's what I want to stick when I find myself steeped in uncertainty, whether physically lost on the side of a mountain or simply unsure of the next choice to make in life. There is perhaps at least a bit of value in being lost in the sense that you are disoriented enough to question where you were originally headed. I'm probably not alone when I admit that where I'm originally headed is not always the best direction to get me to where I need to be. Sometimes I push forward blindly just so I can say I'm headed somewhere and that I'm not actually lost. That I know where I'm going after all. I forget to let myself bask in the unknowing, in the disconcerting feeling of not having a map and the exhilaration of letting the stream lead the way.

I don't always want to feel lost, and I certainly don't want to be lost again on the side of a mountain in a storm anytime soon. But I do want to use those times when I am unsure of where to go next as a channel for going toward the source. I want to let being lost, when it happens, come over me like a vapor, and I want to breathe it in and let it nourish me like a tonic.

When those blue-hued hills give way to grassland again, and they always do, I am reminded that what I want can often be fulfilled in ways that are less flashy than I think they need to be or in ways that I wouldn't choose of my own accord.

The desire to move forward or to make a change isn't without its accompanying challenges. Charting a course isn't a straightforward endeavor. Wayfinding can include feeling lost. Staying aware of what's under our desire for change keeps us moving, even if it's one step forward, two steps back.

Observing Yourself

What would happen if you observed your patterns without judgment?

How adept are you at stepping outside yourself and observing your own patterns? Think of this as mindfulness 2.0. I get the sense this is something many people don't put a lot of energy into, either because life has them in survival mode or there are too many other things distracting their awareness away from what's going on internally. I can't say I'm always fantastic at observing my inner life either, but it's something that I'm actively practicing. It's quite illuminating, really. It's both fascinating and maddening to observe yourself following a current that you know may well take you right over a waterfall, and yet even knowing this, you still hit what feels like an invisible barrier when you try to shift the pattern and respond differently. Just like anything, it gets easier with practice. Sometimes I can respond differently. Sometimes I can't. It takes continual practice and lots of self-compassion. I don't feel like I know what I'm doing or that I'm making any progress half the time. Turns out there's a bit of an art to observing yourself.

Have you ever started making something, maybe a painting or a wool hat or a bookshelf, or even when trying to eat healthier or exercise more, and at some point you get to a place where it seems much easier to set the project down rather than continue to work on it? So often it's tempting to say, "Well, this isn't going well. It's simply not worth it to put in any more effort." So you put the project down. You no longer have to worry about messing it up, but you also don't give yourself the chance to learn something from the process.

Practicing mindfulness in the form of introspection is similar. You try really hard to step outside your thoughts, your reactions, your deeply ingrained tendencies to respond in a certain way, and then it gets too hard. It is frustrating to continually go down those old rutted paths—and it's almost worse to consciously observe yourself doing it, right? It's exhausting in a whole new way. It would be much less painful to go back on autopilot.

However, isn't it more exhausting (in the long run) to be continually swept away in your own current of patterns that has let you down time and time again? To allow yourself to sink into those old ruts that you know will catch you, even if they leave you battered and bruised shortly thereafter? It can feel like those old ruts, those riptides composed of old programming and childhood wounds and cultural bias, are a lifeboat. There is, of course, something to be said for going with the flow and letting fluidity into your life. But there is also something to be said for being able to pull yourself out of a current when you need to, in being able to swim the other way instead of just letting that self-abusive raft carry you away on a river of clouded vision. Not all rivers take you where you need to go, even if you've been on the same one for the last forty-five years. Sometimes you need to portage, or walk upstream, or take a break from the water entirely to get your bearings.

The term *neurodivergent*, which is sometimes abbreviated as ND, describes an individual who has a brain that functions in ways that diverge significantly from the dominant societal standards of "normal." People who identify as neurodivergent are diagnosed or self-diagnosed with things like attention-deficit hyperactivity disorder, autism, dyslexia, dyspraxia, dyscalculia, Tourette syndrome, dissociative disorders, obsessive-compulsive disorder, and anxiety disorders. My friend and fellow nature connection advocate Alissa didn't realize she was neurodivergent until her late thirties. The natural world has been her therapeutic relief since she was a small child, so she founded a community group online for others who have found similar healing in nature. After years of observing things about herself that didn't fit neatly into what society has deemed "normal" when it comes to mental functioning, it's been a relief to acknowledge this in herself and connect with others who also find solace by getting outside and into a natural environment.

Accepting yourself as you are is hard, just like making art or music or other creative projects is hard. Making changes to your lifestyle or your personal expectations of yourself is hard too. Making changes to how you interact with your family, community, or the dominant cultural narrative? Also hard. But when you keep doing hard things, practicing and trying again, you get something back, even if it doesn't always look how you thought it would.

Observing is hard work. You will be swept away on the clouded river time and time again. It's okay. Every time it happens, you have another chance to practice pulling yourself out of the current. When you keep doing it and practicing and trying again, you get something back: yourself. Even if you look different than you thought you would.

Observing the Wild

What does the wildness right outside your door have to teach you?

Kevin Park is someone I worked with several years ago at a nature connection organization that he and Alissa (whom you met in the last chapter) founded, called We Are Wildness.[1] Their mission was, and continues to be, connecting humans with their wild roots and cultivating a love of nature. Because you take care of what you love. Kevin once said, "Rewilding doesn't mean living in caves, gathering all your food, or demonizing human society. It's about reconnecting with Nature—and yourself—in meaningful ways." This way of thinking about the world has become foundational for me. With every step I take further into what rewilding means in my life, the more I'm convinced that *rewilding* is another way to say *simplifying*. To get by with what I have and lessen my contributions to the growth of the economy since we live on a finite planet. To be content with enough. To be where I am, physically and mentally, more often than not.

The squirrels who make their homes in the trees around my house do not have closets full of clothes that are worn far too infrequently to warrant their long tenure or quick replacement. The wild ramps and bloodroot that grow abundantly on the shady hillsides of the ravine in the spring only take in the sustenance that they need. The water lilies that pop-up midsummer around the marshy shallows of the lake don't use cosmetics to enhance what they already are. The vegetables and fruits that we cultivate and harvest from the garden as summer fades into autumn don't continually update their growing protocols to be more productive (even though sometimes I wish they would). The ice crystals that clothe the branches of the ash trees in the depths of winter don't worry about being trendy. They just are what they are, unapologetically.

The wild creatures of land, water, and air who share our soil, our waterways, and our skies as they make their homes on earth use only what they need. They don't seek things out unless they are truly going to use them. A squirrel who hoards acorns gets no judgment from me; he's going to feast on those acorns all winter long. I hoard jars of home-canned tomatoes, and I feel okay about that. Those acorns and tomatoes are life-giving. As a whole, the world could use more things that are life-giving and, to use a buzzword of our time, sustainable.

As birds move through their migration cycles, as a mother fox nurtures her young, and as the basswood trees nourish their roots, they live rooted in a simplicity that can only be found in wildness. Of all the versions of life on earth, humans are some of the only creatures who seem to crave excess and who have a tendency to pursue overabundance, optimization, and ever-growing productivity no matter what the cost.

There is a chipmunk who frequents the space between the woods and the patio outside of my home office door. Most days he darts across the patio from behind the rock pile next to the house and stops abruptly to pick up a seed. Looking around, he takes a few sniffs of the air. Then he nibbles diligently with his tiny hands turning the seed to his liking and stores it away in his cheek to finish later. This goes on for a few moments until he has a full cheek, and then he's off to the rock pile again. I would wager a guess that my resident chipmunk tastes all of the seeds he chews—in those moments there on the patio, eating is what he is doing, so eating is what matters to him. Eating that seed gets the whole of his attention. And those few seconds when he stops to sniff with his nose tuned into the breeze? I bet he is breathing that air with his whole being, taking in the scent of the moment as it unfolds.

Douglas Wood, in a tiny book called *Breathe the Wind, Drink the Rain*,[2] suggests that it's best to "taste what you eat, and smell what you breathe." Sounds like simple advice, right? I thought so too. Then I started to really practice Mr. Wood's advice. It can be more challenging than we think it ought to be to truly taste what we eat and smell what we breathe. The events of the day are really good at commandeering my attention and pulling it into whatever is shouting loudest. Much of the time, we humans eat, breathe, walk, and converse in a state of distraction. Especially when we're "getting things done."

Wild creatures, like my chipmunk neighbor, have a way of living in the present that humans too often neglect to nurture. Sure, muskrats and squirrels don't have bills to pay or papers to file or clients to meet like we do. But they do have bodies to sustain and lives to live. Just like we do.

So I got to thinking, *Okay, how can I be more like my wild neighbors and let my attention be in one place at a time? How can I let wildness lead?*

Easier said than done, but when multitasking is threatening to splice my attention into little bits or I am tempted to sacrifice too much at the altar of efficiency, I try to remember to do a few simple things. When I can remember to do these simple things, I can honestly say that I am present in my moments. That I taste and smell and see and hear and feel with my whole being.

First things first: If I'm not already outside, I open the door and go out. Even if it's cold, cloudy, or raining. There is something about connecting with fresh air that forces me to focus on the present moment.

Then I touch something wild—something that is earth or close to it. Maybe it's a hand on tree bark or bare feet in the garden soil. Maybe it's slipping into the icy-cold water of the lake on a sweltering day or lying on the grass. Maybe it's smelling the wildflowers in the field next door or noticing the icy wind on my face in winter. Direct physical contact with nature is essential to well-being. It grounds me to reality in a way that nothing else can.

Next, I close my eyes. When my eyes are closed, I am forced to rely on something other than sight. I can tune in to the vibrations of a sandhill crane's call as it flies overhead or the feel of a sunbeam on my upturned face. I can taste a raindrop that rolls off of my cheek as it journeys toward the earth. Relying on the other senses plants me directly in the center of presence.

Finally, I look all the way up. Maybe I open my arms wide to the sky. Being rooted in wildness means cultivating the capacity to take up the space that is mine to embody yet also to let go and accept my own smallness in this vast universe. I drink in the open sky and notice the way the wind rustles tree branches. I step fully into my place in Mary Oliver's wild family of things.

When I do these simple things, I come back to earth—to my origin—in a way that honors each moment as it happens. I have rewilded the moment.

I'm not saying we need to give up enjoying the things of daily living that bring joy to being human, like a wonderfully cooked meal, living in a house that has indoor plumbing, owning musical instruments, wearing makeup, or learning how to do a task more effectively. I'm not saying we need to strive to live a life stripped of nothing but the barest essentials needed to stay alive or that we need to mimic the living styles of woodland wildlife. But we can learn from those wild things with whom we share this earth, and we can embrace every opportunity that leads to living a life punctuated by the contentment that comes from letting go of what we don't truly need and finding satisfaction with what we already have.

Walking through Myth

Which myths need to be unraveled?

Walking slowly down a rocky trail in woods that seem to be breathing, I keep stopping to peer more closely at tiny plants and listen to the running water bubbling through the area in a maze of spring-fed streams en route to the larger St. Croix River. The forest floor has a carpet of hepatica, trillium, bloodroot, Dutchman's breeches, and bellwort, a tangle of white, purple, yellow, and green as spring blooms open with the season. Adolescent skunk cabbage and uncurling ferns cast a tint of green as far as the eye can see, everything reaching toward the sun's nourishment. It's like a fairy tale woodland, and I find myself thinking that if there is such a thing as an enchanted forest, this must be it.

This trail is one of several in a local nature preserve. Years ago, one of the park volunteers dubbed this particular pathway the Trail of Myths, and there is a certain energy here that invites questioning those unhelpful stories we talked about earlier—the myths that present in the form of false notions or mistaken beliefs. It's a place requiring honesty, like the upstandingness of a blooming marsh marigold, bold and beautiful even there in the boggy parts of the forest that are too muddy to visit without courageous intention. A place to question and observe and take part in the true story that is being told with every passing moment, no matter what that moment presents. A place to look through myth into truth.

Ever since I lost a long-held corporate job, even though it was years ago, I think more than I would care to admit about money. Is there enough, how can there be just a little bit more, what expenses can be cut? What changes are required so there is *always* enough? Even after getting a new job, publishing some books, and continuing to simplify, the myth of money tells a story that is seductive: that it buys happiness, that having a little more would be better, that it is the source of life, that it could vanish in the blink of an eye. Next to money sits the myths of connectivity and growth: that it's important to be vigilant and always connected, lest an opportunity be missed, always striding with confidence outside the comfort zone. Be afraid of missing out. All or nothing. Growth mindset or death. Attention and economy have melded—and not always for good.

Fortunately, this path through the forest reminds me of the wealth I hold in the form of time and access to wildness (which, of course, is a privilege as well): abundant trails just down the road, a National Scenic Riverway close by, the woodlands and marshes that also call this part of earth home. It reassures me that simply living in a way that makes me feel alive is good enough. That there is a time for growth, but there is also a time for stillness and decline. We could also call this *the myth of scarcity*, and it taunts with the allure of acquiring more: money, comfort, knowledge, validation—even if it means at a cost to time and access to wild spaces. It's the myth that says, "No. Just living? Come on now. Just living is never enough. You have to always be striving. Growing. Reaching higher. Receiving praise in abundance." Gentle reassurance from the forest sometimes wins out over taunts from what author Daniel Quinn called "Mother Culture," but the choice of where to put my attention can be hard to make. Fantasy and fairy tale keep close quarters.

There's something about sitting with moss or hopping over a rock-strewn creek to examine a tiny pink blossom that tells another tale, and it's a storyline that aches to be followed more often. It's the story of a person who lives a life steeped in noticing, a person who moves through days in a slow and intentional way. This person knows when to unplug from the machine to walk through waist-high prairie grass. This person pauses to look up at the sky on days when unplugging isn't realistic. This person accepts hardships and muddles through whatever spectrum of emotion is needed. It's a story that is more parable, less delusion. More fable, less fallacy. A fairy tale maybe—but a believable one. The world could use more believable fairy tales.

Any trail of myths, no matter what the story, is long and winding, full of chances to wonder. There's always something more to want, something more to achieve. Emotions are tempting to dodge if they aren't desired. The twin allure of constant growth and 24/7 digital connection is as persistent as it is exhausting. The modern myths surrounding money and new technologies are not fairy tales, no matter how much the protagonist acquires, no matter how much attention is spliced in the name of productivity, no matter how glossy the cover of the storybook.

There was a time years ago, in college, when I thought, *When I have a job and am out on my own, that'll be enough.* A few years later, sitting in my work cubicle during the day or in my studio apartment in the evenings, I thought, *When I live in a real house and have a family, that'll be enough.* A few years later, gazing out the window of my little urban cottage, sitting across from my new spouse, I thought, *When I live in a house in the country, on a lake, and hear nothing but birdsong in the morning, that'll be enough.* Several years after that, newly laid off, staring at Monster.com on my computer screen, toddler at my feet and birds chirping in abandon, I thought, *When I find a new job, that'll be enough.* And just this year, as I work a pretty stable job from home in my kitchen, sliding door to the back open, birdsong in full spring jubilation as the sun glints off the water, still I think, *When I can make just a little bit more money, fix a few more things on the house, figure out how to balance all these new technologies that want my attention, and not have to work so many hours at my day job, that'll be enough.* Enough can be elusive.

As I round the bend near the halfway point on the Trail of Myths loop, I stop again, this time to examine an outcropping of mushrooms that has popped up on an enormous, decaying, moss-covered stump. White trillium dances in the breeze as warm air lifts hair from my neck, and I think to myself, *When I can figure out how to truly appreciate the experience of a spring woodland, that'll be enough.*

One internal myth that's common for many is that contentment and satisfaction will be just around the next corner. Yet there's always another corner. There is no arriving one day, finally satisfied, finally worry free, finally perfectly balanced, finally in the desired place. There is just each moment as it unfolds. There is just being present to experience the days, no matter what might still seem lacking. No matter how often what seems like enough shifts to longing.

It is a tangled trail, but when I can believe that doing the good work of living is enough, *it is.* When I live and work in ways that fill me up, even when circumstances are challenging, jobs are lost, new jobs don't pay all of the bills, thoughts around money feed fears, technology splices attention into little bits, and the thought of growing even one more inch is too exhausting to fathom, just living is *still enough.* When I operate from a foundation of compassion for self and others, when I accept with tenderness my own vulnerabilities, when I look failure in the eye and see it not as a deep well of despair but a chance to shift course or add another layer of resiliency, then that good work, that way of living *is enough.* Some trails lead toward myths that help me lean into what is enough for a life well lived, and some trails don't. I intend to stay on the route toward wholehearted aliveness, always returning to it when I find myself stumbling down an unmarked trail into thorns.

In this midwestern forest, a humble woodland trail has the power to unravel the myth of not being enough. It challenges the myth of never arriving, and it challenges the myth of finally getting there. After all, there is no arriving—there is only the journey and being present for it. If there ever was an enchanted forest, this must surely be it.

Unlearning to Course Correct

What beliefs do you have (about yourself or the world) that need to be challenged?

The lake ice was just barely holding on after a night of below-freezing temperatures when I noticed my daughter, still in her PJs, transfixed on something out the back sliding door. I followed her gaze, and there they were: three slick brown creatures, slipping and sliding, jumping in and out of the water, scampering across the ice that would hold their weight. We see beavers regularly out on the lake, but these weren't beavers. Every once in a while, earlier that year, someone would see something and say, "Hey, I think that might be an otter," but no one was ever sure, to the point of them being dubbed the "mythical beasts of the lake." Do they exist? Did we just imagine them? What *is* that animal down there who seems way more playful than a muskrat? Having otters this close to home seemed so unlikely. Yet there they were.

Just before noticing the goings-on down on the lake that autumn in 2020, I'd been sorting the pile of mail on the counter—plucking what we actually needed to look at from ad after ad for people running for various offices, from the presidency to the local school board. Just holding political ads makes my body tense up. Something about the energy presented, the "I'm better than that other person and this is why" triggers overwhelm and anxiety.

As Election Day loomed during a pandemic that showed no signs of letting up after a wildfire season that included the biggest blaze in Colorado's history, it was tempting to keep refreshing my news tabs and tweet and comment and scroll until my eyes bugged out. What could go wrong next? There was a lot swirling around out there. Much of it wasn't (and still isn't) good news. Everything wants attention, and everyone wants to ensure everyone else knows they're on the right side of history. Communities were divided (and still are), and tension was high (and still is). Neighbors stole one another's signs. I felt both easily distracted and hyper-focused.

When you take a moment to consider the state of the world, it's easy to feel like humanity is pointed in the wrong direction. Reading the headlines or even looking down the street, sometimes it seems like the world is set to collapse in paradox at any moment. It's possible to read an article about what an Olympic figure skater plans to do next followed by one about North Korea's nuclear plans followed by one about a recent extreme weather event followed by one about the pros and cons of the latest smartphone to hit the market. The information overload can be paralyzing.

And when stuck in overload mode, it can be really hard to wrap your mind around what can possibly be done to help yourself, much less impact the world for good. So why bother? Might as well just get that latest smartphone and see what the Kardashians are up to, right?

Consumer culture would have us believe that is surely the answer—read all the big headlines, throw our hands up, and go buy something. Do what we need to do to get through the day. I've certainly felt that way before, even though I really don't like immersing myself in the news or shopping in any form.

That's what many folks have internalized. Yet the mind doesn't have the capacity to contain such an onslaught of information every single day. We live on a finite planet that can't sustain infinite growth, even if we are taught that growth is essential for the health of the economy. That's not to say that we should ignore what's happening; that won't get us anywhere either. We need to dig deeper into the root of this split (both with our inner selves and with those who are different than us) that's permeating the world. What if we could heal the separation? What if we could unlearn some of what's gotten us into some of these messes in the first place?

Several years ago, writer Charles Eisenstein introduced me to the idea of the space between stories by way of an online multiweek course of the same name. He described it as a time of figuring out what it means to be human on an earth that is struggling in myriad ways: from climate change to wealth inequality to health disparities to racism to war to freshwater scarcity . . . the list could go on and on. The space between stories, according to Eisenstein, "is the time when the old story of who we are, what is real and how to navigate has essentially broken down. It's a time when familiar ways of making meaning and operating in day-to-day life are no longer relevant. And it's a time when, every now and then, even through the darkest of times, glimpses of what could be present themselves."[1]

Activist Jodie Evans spoke during one of the course sections, and she shared stories about her work in standing up for nonviolent communication efforts, protests against various war activities, and her experiences from a life spent working to promote local peace economies. She's an advocate of not forcing an outcome but of instead taking action that aligns with her values and being okay with not knowing what might come to pass as a result. She bases her work on cultivating hope from the soil of positive change, regardless of scale. I was moved and inspired when she said, "Be in the conversation, not the fight." In her work, she has seen firsthand how operating from a place of love, even when the outcome is completely unknown (and acting from love seems too risky), has proven infinitely more effective than simply going to battle for a cause.

It can be challenging to interact with people these days. People often don't agree, resistance to listening to differing points of view is common, and fear tends to underlie communication, especially in the media. People, myself included, can be pre-contemplative about making any sort of change to current lifestyles or ways of thinking about the world. We can be up in arms because we feel forced to do things in life that seem either like jumping through hoops or like joining a losing battle—from keeping a job to getting a promotion to putting food on the table.

Sometimes people we know and respect come into a conversation ready to fight: with us, with the committee, with the employer, with the system. Sometimes *we* go into an interaction—with our leaders, with our colleagues, with our family members, even with ourselves—expecting a fight. Inertia in the direction you're trying to shift away from can feel like an unbeatable foe after years of trying to force a desired outcome into being, no matter how worthy the cause. Being in a fight is usually short-lived—you take and throw some punches, and eventually someone limps or is carried away. Not much gets solved.

On the other hand, being in a conversation takes staying power. Compassion. Empathy for "the other." It takes deep listening and seeing from someone else's perspective. In a fight, it's everyone with blinders on going to battle for what they think is right. In a conversation, it's seeing through the eyes of the other and then acting from love despite a difference of belief or opinion or status. It's being open to new ways of existing alongside things that make us uncomfortable. Being in a conversation doesn't have to mean compromising on something that goes against what you value deep in your bones, but it does mean acting from considering the question "what is it like to be you?" when interacting with your conversation partner. It's important to note that there is privilege involved in having the capacity to choose a conversation over a fight: folks from marginalized groups often don't have many opportunities to make this choice. There are times when a fight is necessary. Yet there are usually opportunities to choose to interact with a situation differently. (This is, of course, much easier said than done.)

There are no easy answers when it comes to solving the problems of the world—that much is obvious. To bring it back to Charles Eisenstein again, he says that to be true agents of change, we don't need "smarter solutions." Instead, he says we need different questions. That we need to unlearn the things we assume we know.

For me, a life that allows course correction requires a continuous willingness to live with discomfort, to be wrong, to have hard conversations, and to discern when to listen, when to pass the mic, and when to speak up. It requires internal struggle. It requires looking for and taking opportunities to pass power held to those who need to be heard.

I mess up and get things wrong, do things wrong, and slip back into old patterns on a regular basis. Once I chose a word with Algonquin origins to use in a book title, and I shouldn't have—the word wasn't mine to claim without permission, even though it resonated with me. There are surely even things in this book that I'll look back on as missteps, from microaggressions that I couldn't identify because of my own bias to fragility that I thought I'd worked through already. As time continues, there will be myriad opportunities to continue to unlearn what growing up white in a culture that rewards whiteness has taught me. I've heard it said in various ways these past few years that "white supremacy isn't the shark: it's the water."[2] Being anti-racist isn't just one piece of personal development. Anti-racism is a deconstruction of the systems of oppression from which I and other white folks benefit. It's taking a hard look at the air we breathe, the food we eat, the education and experiences we provide our children, the entertainment and media we consume, the books and art we enjoy, the stories we tell. It requires us to turn a critical eye to how we live and make adjustments. Many people want to be thought of as a good ally. So do I. And I've learned that just like you don't simply one day arrive at your anti-racism destination, ally status isn't something you achieve and get to keep on your shelf. Allyship isn't an identity I can assign myself—it's something I need to earn over and over again, day after day after day. It's a muscle you've got to flex to keep it in shape. It's hard, humbling, and necessary work.

I often find myself wanting to be seen as doing the right thing, to be on the "right side of history," and that very desire is problematic because it puts me in the center. It puts making myself look or feel better as the motivation instead of justice and peace for all. That desire gets momentum going, but it doesn't have the legs for the long haul. Fortunately, with practice and a critical but self-compassionate eye, I can keep searching for my own bias and selfish motivations, and when I find them, keep them in the spotlight, where they dissolve little by little. I can keep coming back to the path and resolve to keep going, no matter what. As Ijeoma Oluo writes, "The beauty of anti-racism is that you don't have to pretend to be free of racism to be anti-racist. Anti-racism is the commitment to fight racism wherever you find it, including in yourself. And it's the only way forward."[3]

There is so much to unlearn to course correct to the path toward true peace and reconciliation. We've got to do it though, no matter how uncomfortable that path gets.

I plan to continue to prioritize the practices that give me life, the things that bring joy and peacefulness. To rest when I need to. But to also keep my eyes open to the wider world and acknowledge my complicity. Peace, joy, and aliveness are only truly possible when everyone can experience them.

For Stacy Bare, a US Army veteran and an old high school classmate of mine, opting outside was a big part of unlearning some maladaptive coping mechanisms he'd been relying on after coming home from Iraq after this second tour. After several years of struggling with survivors' guilt and substance abuse, he credits outdoor re-creation, from climbing to dog sledding to surfing, as why he was able to shift the trajectory of his life from hurting others and himself to helping other veterans cope with their trauma and reclaiming his own joy. In 2015, Stacy founded Adventure Not War, with the mission of promoting peace through outdoor adventures. A twenty-five-minute documentary of the same name highlights his and two other veterans' trip to climb and ski 11,834-foot Mount Halgurd, the highest peak entirely in Iraq. They returned to areas where they once fought to interact with the landscape in a way that invited healing instead—to carve through fresh powder instead of taking up arms in battle. Today, Stacy's work with an organization called Happy Grizzly Adventures[4] focuses on helping individuals foster better mental health by getting outside, practicing mindfulness, and having the sort of conversations that lead to inner peace rather than outer turmoil. He has been unlearning what war taught him. He course corrected to the path that invites peace and reconciliation (with himself and others) instead.

I'm still in the unlearning process, and always will be, but here are a few questions that come to my mind as important: How can we be in the conversation but not the fight? What would it take to be in that place of unknowing and still hold space for conversations that foster hope and, ultimately, invite the change that will lead to a more beautiful world? What actions truly hold BIPOC lives as more important than white feelings? How can combat veterans live lives of beauty and peace even after what they've been through? And when I take this line of questioning closer to home: What are my blind spots from privilege? What am I willing to give up for true liberation of BIPOC folks? What about giving up privilege makes me uneasy? According to Jodie Evans, part of what will help is letting go of the "right answer" and making sure to operate from what we know deep down as truth. That truth might be different than we thought. Apologizing for wrongs is important, yet an apology is hollow until behaviors are changed. Talking about and getting support with post-traumatic stress disorder is important, and so is embracing the activities (and getting the necessary support) that'll allow full presence to the good things in life instead of being stuck in past traumas or current anxieties.

There's much to be said for working for a cause you believe in, advocating for justice, being informed, taking a stand, and speaking up. A global community calls for all hands on deck, sails raised to catch the wind needed to propel the world toward the changes necessary for peace. There's a lot of high wind right now, and it's hard to know which way to steer the ship. It's hard to keep the kind of loose yet confident grip on the wheel that keeps a vessel moving in the right direction. Yet when we live our lives in ways that tell the truth, we're better equipped to discern where our opportunities are for ways to enter the conversation instead of going to battle.

Conversations so often begin because someone takes a risk. It's grace and a willingness to engage in a peaceful way (peaceful doesn't mean without challenge and risk) that allows a misstep to become part of the healing process rather than another call to arms. A lot of questions may remain unanswered. There is no one right way to navigate these waters, and that's because the conversation, wherever it leads, is the way through.

As Stacy told me when we connected in the autumn of 2021, "We seek the one thing we can point to, or understandably grab ahold of, to help us explain what is going wrong—at war, I saw people die, so that was the issue. Since it didn't kill me, it allowed me to enter into conversation with myself, my community, and my own history to come out the other side, if not more anxious and rawer, maybe a little stronger."

Taking care of the self, by whatever means work for each of us, is essential when it comes to embarking on this path of truly unlearning in order to course correct. We can't do the necessary work when we are depleted and burnt out. We can't do the necessary work when we get stuck in guilt and fragility. And when you live steeped in privilege like I do, it's easy to stop if you aren't feeling good: if you need a break, if things start feeling out of control, if you don't know what to do next. Sometimes it feels like I've been wrestling with my privilege and how to make a positive difference for a long time, but in reality, I've only begun scratching the surface. Activism makes me uncomfortable, just as much as I feel called to do more of it. Thinking about going to protests or marches, or about being in large crowds of folks, or about taking a stand at a school board meeting to advocate for social justice, or about using my physical body as a barrier to stop something from happening and getting arrested makes my heart rate go up. I fall short of what I'd like to see myself doing on a regular basis. I have lots of ideas on how to get involved and make a difference but less practical follow-through. However, social anxiety and trouble with large crowds, and the fact that I will probably never be the person up front with the megaphone, do not give me a pass; it means I need to find the ways to advocate and speak up that are the most effective and sustainable. Writing letters to governing bodies, voting in local elections, providing behind-the-scenes support for those on the frontlines, talking to my daughter about what's going on in the world, amplifying the voices of those groups that need to be listened to, and being present in my immediate community are all things that I *can* do and will continue to push myself to do more consistently.

Sometimes moving forward means looking directly at the hard stuff, getting broken down and built back up again as you claw your way out of the darkness. And there are days when moving forward means hitting pause to notice some wild animals frolic and splash. Taking a break from hard conversations about complex issues to engage with wildness is often the antidote I need to shift from overwhelm to awe. To loosen my grip enough to roll with the waves, even if those waves are coming at me because of my own mistakes. Part of self-care must be rest and replenishment, but it must be the sort that readies you for action, not the sort that lures you away from hard questions and truth. Unlearning requires hard, humbling work.

That chilly morning, those otters were mythical beasts no more, and we gazed upon their playtime as the sun rose higher, slowly melting the rest of the ice. They invited me to set the heaviness of the times down for a little while and take up a different path instead. They helped me correct my course just enough to look for the next opportunity to enter the conversation in a life-giving way.

I'm convinced a balance of looking at the hard things along with plenty of time paying attention to the natural world will help us tap into the questions and the truths that might just lead to the changes the world needs most.

Embodying What's Yours

How do you feel about how you are taking up space?

Water goes where it feels like going: it flows and seeps and gushes where it wants, regardless of what anyone thinks of it. It takes up the space in which it fits best, and it doesn't apologize for doing so. Water is always at the edge of where it wants to go. Humans can take a cue from this—to fully embody our sense of self, our sensuality, and our humanity, we have to go to our edges. We have to take up all of the space that we are meant to take up. But not more. We can't step into someone else's.

Our sense of self comes, in large part, from the relationship we have with our physical body. Emotional and spiritual health play a part, of course, but we humans are sensual beings, and sensuality is tied to the physical. After all, the body is our gateway to experiencing life and all the pleasures and pains that come with it. Sensuality is also an agreement we make with ourselves, one that defines how we show up in the space that is ours.

Thanks to twenty years immersed in the realm of health and wellness, I have worked with a lot of people who are seeking transformation. They want something different. And they tend to echo each other.

> *I want to feel good in my skin.*
> *I want to feel confident in my appearance.*
> *I want to have more energy.*
> *I want to keep up with my children, my job, my life.*
> *I want to take up space in a way that feels right and good.*
> *I want to feel good so I can do good.*

People rarely say those last two verbatim, but it's what I hear beneath what they're saying. It's a common human desire to feel like we matter, to feel like we are doing what we want to be doing. We all want to feel like we have the confidence we need to live the life we have been given and use our life energy for what feels right to us.

Claiming who you are, like we discussed earlier, is one thing and an essential step. Taking up space fully, no matter how you define yourself, is another. And taking up space as your true self can be a very scary thing, especially when you allow yourself to really be there and feel all of the nuances that come from doing so.

Sometimes when I'm sitting on the couch, listening to the clock tick, I wonder if I am afraid of silence, of being idle, of stillness. Of taking up space without doing anything in particular. I always encourage others to cultivate that empty space—that quiet well—for themselves, but do I do it for myself? The pull to constantly be reading or figuring out a problem or checking for a message or writing a blog post or vacuuming the rugs or making something better, or cleaner, or more worthwhile . . . the pull to be productive in some form—to be doing something always—is strong. Sometimes (who am I kidding?—*almost always*) it's strong enough that I give in to the pull, the allure of constant engagement or stimulation or value creation. Proof of worth. Validation that I am thinking or doing important things that matter. Ensuring I am making something of myself. Being the one who always knows the answer or who can figure it out or refer you to someone who can. Taking up space in ways that show I am worthy of the space I'm inhabiting.

I try to remind myself that I don't need to be the one who knows the answer all the time. Trying to do that is kind of like trying to step into someone else's space, but letting go of it feels scary. Vulnerability is an essential part of being a well-rounded human, but being truly vulnerable is harder in practice than just writing about how important it is to be vulnerable. And for many, especially LGBTQIA2+ or BIPOC folks, being vulnerable can be especially risky given the potential for physical harm that comes with it.

Sitting in stillness and embracing the silence of being idle takes practice, and when something that seems so simple is so challenging, it's harder to keep practicing it. It's easier to say, "Be okay with not always being okay" than it is to actually live by that advice. It's harder still when one is dealing with trauma, no matter what the cause. Yet we don't have to have everything figured out. It's okay to exist as an imperfect, flawed being and to be confused about where your edges are. Seeking out practice wisdom in all of its messy and uncomfortable nuances and ensuring we keep hold of our priorities (as well as getting the support of a therapist when needed!) helps keep that old temptress, *worthiness*, from running away with our sense of self. There are times when old, tired scripts need to fade so new lines that feel better can have room to bloom.

When I was a high school gymnast, the team didn't have a dedicated practice area. There was a balance beam set up in the empty space at one end of the gymnasium, along with a shorter practice beam, and a few mats stacked on top of each other. Another full-size beam with a crash mat underneath filled the rest of the area. At the other end of the gym was the wrestling mat we used for floor routines and two sets of uneven bars. In between the equipment and the basketball court was the netting we set up right after school ended every day—gymnastics season was also boys basketball season, and they had practice at the same time. This netting was supposed to keep us safe.

Before starting apparatus practice, we warmed up by jogging around the perimeter of the basketball court, the whole team in various hues of leotards and spandex shorts with the waists rolled down. No one wore T-shirts, even though some of us wanted to. We stretched, did some more warm-up drills, and broke into groups; one group went to bars on the far side of the gym and the other to the beam. I climbed onto the four-inch surface and tried to concentrate on my handstand instead of the sound of basketballs bouncing.

Instead of the appraising gaze that came from the court now and then. Part of me wished I had a T-shirt on. Part of me wanted to be seen.

In high school and early college, smallness was good. To excel in gymnastics (and long-distance running, which I also did), a small body is an asset. So is strength, which I also wanted, but in those days, I wanted the smallness just as much. Probably more. The uniforms for both sports are tiny and tight. I didn't want to take up too much space, and I wanted to feel worthy of the space that I did fill. There was something unnerving about being seen, even when I wanted it. Most of the time I didn't really know what I wanted. I wasn't sure where my edges were.

Fast forward about five years later. When I was about a year out of college, I worked at a wilderness camp high in the northern Colorado Rockies. Mid-May at nine thousand feet meant there was still plenty of snow on the trails. That year, the snowpack held firm above the tree line for weeks after I arrived. Five of us packed some backpacks, grabbed some trekking poles, and set off, glad to be moving and gaining elevation. Crossing snowfield after snowfield, we picked our way higher and higher until we reached Emmaline Lake, an alpine oasis nestled at the base of a range of peaks that is known as the Mummy. It took a few falls through high drifts and some scratches to arms and legs as we inched along a rocky ledge, but finally we made it to the water's edge. The lake was perfectly calm and still iced-over in spots. We walked along the boulder-strewn perimeter up to a smaller lake that was just off the trail proper. This one held shimmering open water. We sat down to eat lunch and bask in the sun.

After lunch, one of my hiking companions, Katie, stood up. She nonchalantly stripped off her hiking clothes and dipped a toe into the crystal-clear, ice-cold water. "What is she doing?" I urgently whispered to Jenn, looking sideways at the two guys who'd come along as well to see if they were paying attention. Katie gave us a coy look over her shoulder and dove in.

Ever since coming to work in the mountains, I wasn't comfortable in my body; I felt like I was taking up too much space in my clothes.

"Aaahhh!" A shirt flew to my right, and Ahmed went in with a yell. So did Mark.

Skinny dipping—that wasn't really something I could do, was it? Other people would see me. I felt safe with this group of people, but I wasn't sure I wanted to take up that kind of space. Wouldn't everyone just be uncomfortable?

I wondered what it would be like to have some of Katie's confidence.

Jenn and I, still fully clothed at the water's edge, exchanged wary glances. I held my breath as we stripped as quickly as possible without making eye contact.

When I ran into that frigid water, I felt my body waking up as the contrast between the water and the powerful Colorado sun made me gasp in exhilarated alarm. Later, drying off on the rocks in the warm midday sun, I took up all the space I needed. I relaxed fully to the edges of my skin.

That afternoon at Emmaline Lake, my body wanted to be immersed in cold water and then gradually dried off on warm rocks in the sun, even though my mind wasn't so sure. I'm glad I gave in to what my body wanted even though it felt hard to do. Jumping into that cold alpine water, feeling the tingling, and enjoying the decadent warmth on the rocks afterward was an act of ingesting beauty, of becoming the mountain, of becoming myself a little bit more. It didn't matter what size or shape my body was to do those things.

Ahmed, always with his camera equipment, snapped a black-and-white photo of our backs as we sat on the rocks after emerging from the water. I still have that photograph, twenty-some years later, in a frame on the wall next to my desk. It's a reminder to give in to what I want (when doing so is life-giving), to take up the space I need to thrive, and feel filled up with goodness. To go to the edges.

There's nothing like an icy-cold dip into an alpine lake on a sunny day after a long hike that reminds you to take up space in a way that feels good. Just like there's nothing like a cozy evening after returning to your home base, spent by the fire, wrapped in a blanket, snuggled up to someone you love. There is something about the contrast of being out in the elements of nature followed by the act of getting cozy and warm inside that can make a person shiver in delight, it's so good. I don't think it's just the feeling of being comfortable after being cold, wet, or windblown—it's being so fully in your body that you allow it to take pleasure in whatever it is experiencing.

Quinn wrestled with stepping out of the socially conditioned norms that had always defined their life to embrace being nonbinary and, by doing so, found exhilaration and excitement in being fully themselves. I had to let go of the socially conditioned norm of having a certain bodily appearance to take off my clothes and jump in a lake in order to have that experience on the mountain. What do you need to let go of to be unapologetically yourself? Even if it's uncomfortable or hard, what would get uncovered if you went there? One of the best places to learn about yourself is somewhere between the tension of what you want and what you need. Allowing yourself to be there allows you to take up the space you're meant to embody. The tension created between risk and self-ownership is essential to fully experience life.

We need to venture to the edges of our skin yet avoid trying to step into someone else's. We need to take up space in a way that feels right and good. We need to be in our bodies, whatever they look like, whatever color or gender or size they are, and let doing so be a gateway to joy, adventure, right action, and everything that comes in between. We need to surrender to the contrast that makes us shiver with delight. We need to own our edges, visit them often, and allow others enough space to do the same.

Embracing Transformation

How has hardship been transformational for you?

Anyone who's lived in the western United States or Canada or Australia has probably experienced, or at least witnessed, the effects of a forest fire. The frequency, size, and intensity of such events have increased significantly in the last several years as the climate continues to shift. Baseline temperatures rise, and conditions change. Insects that used to die off in colder climates no longer do so and eat their way through the pine forests, turning the mountainsides red that fades to gray. I worked at Sky Ranch, the camp mentioned in the last chapter, in the northern Rockies of Colorado in 2003, and the landscape is completely different now than it was then as the lodgepole pines meet their demise in the form of a tiny insect, the pine beetle. At camp and in all the other areas where this is happening, other than manually removing the trees (which is not practical for most situations), the only remedy is fire. But with the

97

increasing popularity of living in the picturesque mountain villages where these beetles now thrive (and feast) that has led to a continually expanding population, fire is not welcome. Fire is the enemy, and it makes sense, doesn't it? If I lived in a mountain town in Colorado, even as I watched my beloved hillsides turn brown and then brittle gray, I wouldn't want them to burn. I wouldn't want to have to flee or watch my neighbors lose their homes. I would want people to be safe and happy and thriving. It was sad to watch those trees at camp get taken down, even though it had to happen. I wanted things to look how they always had. After all, I had good memories from that place.

The catch is that I also want my beloved forest to be happy and thriving. Skeletal trees left to act as silent sentries don't conjure up feelings of "thriving" in my mind. When the trees die, the forest needs transformation. It needs change. It needs a blast of energy to invite newness to enter into its realm. It needs fire.

Philip Connors wrote, "Smokey Bear's message—that fire was to be stamped out always and everywhere—represents one of the most successful public relations campaigns in American history."[1] Threats of fire invoke fear into most humans. And it makes sense, right? If there was a fire coming at your village, you'd be scared. I'd be scared. I'd want to put the fire out.

My parents met at Sky Ranch in the 1970s. They each worked there several seasons. My dad guided campers to summit Hagues Peak, a 13,573-foot thirteener. He was the only staffer on site with any medical training the time a visiting group made the ill-advised decision to slide down some snowfields only to crash into rocky scree fields, leaving some with injuries serious enough they had to be airlifted out. They worked with Ruth, and Leon, and Dan, and Bob, people who are still in their lives today. My folks took me there when I was a toddler, and we sat on a bridge over Beaver Creek, one of the streams that runs through the property. The Stormy Peaks trail hosted them and my twin brothers on a backpacking trip in the early 1990s, while my other brother and I went whitewater rafting further west with my grandparents. They took me and a group of other high school youth on a backpacking trip in 1996, and we spent a day in silence walking across Sugarloaf Mountain, bushwhacked our way from the mouth of the Poudre River to Mirror Lake (leaving no trace, of course), and relished cold cans of soda from a Pingree Park (Colorado State University's mountain campus) vending machine when we came off the trail a week later. My future spouse and I spent an unplanned night on the side of Mummy Mountain once in a storm. When I was on staff there, I was the camp naturalist. I have hiked or started pack trips from camp countless times. My daughter's middle name is Emmaline, after the alpine lake near camp. It's been harder to visit in the last several years for myriad reasons, but the Comanche Peak Wilderness and the trails that lead away from Sky Ranch will always feel like one of my "home forests."

In October of 2020, the Cameron Peak fire, the largest in Colorado state history at this writing, burned through camp. The lodge, cabins, and historic buildings survived thanks to the tireless efforts of wildland firefighters, but the landscape that I know and love has been irrevocably changed.

Conners goes on to describe his work as a fire sentry in the mountains of New Mexico. He recounts hearing a manager say, "Every fire is a birthday for the next forest." And despite the stigma and the fear around fire, he began to "see that a burned forest has a beauty of its own."

It's like that in our own lives too. Sometimes when we are stuck in a rut, completely unsure where to move next in life, the only thing that creates the movement we need to thrive again is fire. When we can embrace the heat, the uncertainty, and the intensity that can come with transition and change, transformation takes place. We evolve into a new way of being in the world that can only arrive because we let something in ourselves burn up and move out. When we can let a fire consume our internal beetles, even though the process can be painful and full of sorrow, we create space in which to shine a light. We invite an opportunity to explore an area that might have otherwise remained unnoticed.

There's a sense of emptiness and mourning that gets left behind after a fire goes through, whether it goes metaphorically through a life or literally through a forest. Sometimes that emptiness allows a new space to be visible. When the old passes away, it points to a gate that leads to the world that lies beyond what we can see clearly at first glance. It's a gate that invites us to open it, walk through, and figure out where we are supposed to go next.

This issue is more complex than simply accepting that forest fires are a part of life, of course. There are real threats to life, livelihood, and communities to be dealt with when wildfires blaze their way into the picture. Human-caused climate disruption makes these fires more likely and more destructive. But perhaps there is something to be learned from the outcome of being forced to deal with the ramifications of transformation.

After a fire burns itself out, the site is black and smells of soot and acridity. It can look pretty bleak for a while. As the months roll on, life slowly returns. And the life there was never totally gone. Under the soil, microbes and rhizomes and roots (even while the surface was scorched away) continued to live. Seeds that need heat to open were granted the gift of life. After a burn, new trees and plants are offered an opportunity to grow now that the sun can reach the ground. Eventually there is a tint of green mixed in with the black, and with the help of a little nourishment, the new seedlings begin to make their way to the light. Wildlife returns, and a new forest is born.

The wind gusted hard here in Minnesota that autumn of the Cameron Peak fire. All the brilliantly colored leaves seemed to swirl to the ground in a matter of hours after one afternoon of high wind. Combines kicked up great clouds of dust as they harvested. Dead vines and rotten fruit were pulled from the garden. A loose piece of siding on the house rattled day after day.

The wind was also gusting hard hundreds of miles away, in that Rocky Mountain pine forest at nine thousand feet. Trees burned. Firefighters defended structures. Animals fled. Residents prayed for respite and safety.

Blustery and uncertain conditions are hard to navigate. They can be unpleasant. They're inconvenient. They can be devastating. They can also offer possibilities.

That autumn at my house, milkweed pods burst open, seeds taking flight.

Any serotinous pine cones in the burning forests released their seeds because of new heat.

We won't know where those seeds landed until they sprout again, but they landed somewhere to take root and grow into something new.

Dousing the Fire (with Love)

*What do you need to give your energy to in order
to fully love?*

Sometimes when I'm working with people, I'll ask them to call out the qualities they like about themselves, and it's almost always hard for them to do that. Has your body (whether the physical one that tends to come to mind first or bodies such as the mental, emotional, or spiritual) ever felt like the enemy? I'm guessing that you, at some point in life, have felt some animosity toward some aspect of your being. Most people do. I certainly have. People seem to default toward sharing what's not working, what they are trying to change, what's got to go. Many of the folks I coach are working through body hatred and a general sense of dissatisfaction. Most folks don't go around proclaiming self-love.

Unprompted, the qualities people like about themselves remain largely unsaid (if they can think of anything at all). From not liking physical appearance to not feeling smart enough to feeling like there's not enough money or prestige or friends, human beings—you, me, and most people—are fantastic at calling out the negative. There is, of course, plenty of negative stuff going on in the world. Feeling bad about yourself, or what's happening in the world that you can't control, can feel like the end of the world.

Not to mention, these days it's really easy to find information on what people think the actual end of the world might look like. Dystopian fiction is one of the most popular genres out there, and sometimes the stories read eerily close to reality, futures often easy to imagine after reading the news. I've read at least fifteen YA novels about everything from the moon crashing into the earth to people synching with technology to the elite living in bubbles while the rest of the world suffers in increasingly harsh natural elements. But there's almost always a love story too.

Anne Herbert, in an essay titled "Handy Tips on How to Behave at the Death of the World," wrote, "Falling in love is appropriate for now, to love all these things which are about to leave. The rocks are watching, and the squirrels and the stars and the tired people in the street. If you love them, let them know, with grace and non-invasive extravagance. [This] is your last chance."[1]

As I first read the essay, which was published in the March 2019 issue of *The Sun*, I assumed she was talking about the planet. You know, how it's dying. After all, the climate is shifting in rapid, probably unchangeable ways at this point in history; storms are bigger and come more regularly; ice is melting; and islands and species are disappearing, all of this largely due to human activity. But then, when I read it again, I also got the sense that she's talking about people, how we tend to treat one another, how -isms have commandeered so much of social interaction, how consumerism has dislocated our self of purpose and meaning. Reading it a third time, she's definitely talking about how we humans tend to treat animals and plants—like something to have dominion over rather than something to relate to with grace and empathy and kinship. But whatever stands out, it's apparent that she's illustrating something important, something to keep close to the bone, something to put into practice using my entire being. Something to remember before it's too late to forget.

What if we could be reminded of all that's there to love? That pebbles, raindrops, grassy meadows, old log cabins high in the back-country, sidewalks that act as homes for those who have nowhere else to go, that latte at your favorite café downtown, a wave to your neighbor each morning on the way to work, robins, alley cats, orange dahlias in various stages of bloom, feedlot cattle, a lone American bison standing watch, red-rock canyons, long-legged spiders, the person next to you on the subway who looks like they haven't had a shower in weeks, high winds, old books, the guy who writes daily letters to his young son from a prison cell, small children who wake up singing, snow gently falling on glassy water in spring, your own body walking the land—that all of this is ours to love, and all of this calls us to use our lives as elegies that aren't yet fully needed but may be someday? Which is all the more reason to use this chance, this life that is each of ours, to actively fall in love with the world, continuously letting the world know how we feel with "grace and non-invasive extravagance."

It's important to keep one foot planted firmly in reality, of course. I'm not saying we should gloss over issues that need to be managed or look for the positive in an unsustainable situation. Engaging in physical activity can be a wonderful avenue toward improving health, studying for a test can help a student learn the material, and having enough money to provide what's needed to sustain a good quality of life in modern culture is part of the story. Getting to the root of a problem, effectively managing anxiety or depression, and identifying what needs to shift are essential. But beating yourself up over what's not working doesn't help anything improve.

Paula D'Arcy wrote, in *Gift of the Red Bird,* "I have taken better care of some of my cars than I have of me. I wouldn't set fire to my home, but I have been willing to set fire to myself."[2] When you continually beat yourself up for not being "enough" of something and push constantly toward what culture or your mom or that little demon on your shoulder says you *should* be, you are, in a sense, setting yourself on fire. When you look at the scale of some of the issues humanity faces, or even just what you'll accomplish in your one human lifetime, thinking, *What I do is never going to make a difference* is a common refrain.

It can be easy to get lost in the flames of betterment, under a grimy layer of self-doubt that's too often laced with a film of self-contempt.

Time to douse the fire.

Ask yourself this: What has my life belonged to? Jot down your answers. Be honest. Some of the things that have gotten pieces of your life won't make you feel good. That's okay. Some of them you'll need to take responsibility for at some point. Some of them are not your fault. Just note them.

The next question is: What do I want to give my life to? Write down your answers again. Be honest. There is no right or wrong;

there are just the things that are calling you into doing something different. Remember to treat yourself with kindness and respect. Self-*love* might feel too hard when you start, and that's okay. Every time you offer yourself a simple gesture of respect, you're a bit closer to being able to go there.

Your body—whether it's your physical body, mental body, spiritual body, or the collective body of humanity of which we're all a part—has been waiting its whole life for this.

Of course, it's worth saying that there's a lot I don't love about the world. The same probably goes for you. There are plenty of words that describe what I don't particularly care for in modern life. It's good to get that out now and then, right? Just to make sure you are on the same page as yourself. My current list of what I don't like goes something like this:

Screens, pavement, harsh lights, clicking, automobiles, fuel oil, business, morebetterfaster, distraction, quality assurance, industrialization, red number 5, processed corn, scrolling, wires, noise, inequality, defeat, white supremacy, competition, colonization, dog racing, banks, media, TV, debt, so many ads, shopping malls, AI, MOA, IKEA, GMOs, plastic, productivity, cancer, the military budget, feed lots, fast food, high heels, the interstate, numbness, apathy, mining, uncomfortable but stylish furniture, airport security, Fitbits, the American health-care system, curating an image, hurrying, feelings of disconnection, isolation, stepping around important issues, toxic positivity.

In coaching, we often discourage folks from focusing on what they don't like, but sometimes I wonder if it can be cathartic to just say it. Just get it out rather than stewing. Set it on the table, not to feed on but to clear it away for something else. To douse anything inflammatory with a pitcher of cold water. Then you can turn your focus to what makes you glad to be alive and breathing. To that which makes you ache with love for the world.

Right now, my "what I love about the world" list goes something like this: owls, rainbows, thunder, moonlight, togetherness, music, gentle sounds, wood, aspen leaves, clear water, pebbles, tomato plants, apple trees, rocky trails, canoes, movement, breath, stillness, snow, faith, room for doubt, bread ovens, birds, foxes, skin on skin, snails, books, healthy soil, gardens, solitude, the scent of pine on a hot day, farmers' markets, pottery, wool, goats, chickens, trust, mountains, jack-in-the-pulpit, fairy houses in old logs, courage, noticing the details, wild swans, deer walking up the hillside as dusk falls on the lake as long as they don't eat the garden, blueberry-stained fingers, belonging, children who see God in unexpected places, fiddlehead ferns uncurling in spring, holding hands, being seen, seeing others, a gasp of delight no matter the reason, red-winged blackbird trills, sandhill cranes, wildflowers in highway ditches, healers, peacemakers, truth tellers, tallgrass prairie, listening, days with no pings, forest creatures rustling leaves, ordinary rituals, wind in white pines, people who really listen, homemade ice cream and cookies, soreness from a day of chopping wood or planting seeds, wood heat, skiing across a frozen lake into the sunrise, baby animals of all sorts, filtered sunlight, feeling all feelings.

I don't like to dwell too long on the list of what I don't like about the world, but I could go on for a long, long time about what makes me ache with love for that very same world. In a culture that spends a lot of time on what's wrong, I want to spend more time on what's beautiful and right. There is much work to be done, yet I'm inclined to think keeping our gaze firmly on the sort of energy that helps a wildflower grow in a ditch between six lanes of pavement is what's going to keep us from despair and inaction. The capacity to notice and respect the gaze of an owl might just be some of the world's best medicine.

I appreciate how writer Chris La Tray put it in the March 19, 2021, installment of his newsletter, *An Irritable Métis*: "It sounds overly sentimental but love can heal the world. Or at least our human place in it. It is the only thing that can! But we have to move beyond the definitions of what love is as just this airy *thing* and create an active love in the world. [It] takes work. Sometimes toil. Sometimes setting aside what is easier, or what we think we want, to show love as courtesy. Love as simple kindness. Love that can be inconvenient. Love that challenges us. If we all did a little more of that, how much better would we get along?"[3]

There will be times when you can't see further than a few feet in front of you, but what if those few feet are enough? Knowing more about the path could change how you travel it, sure. But then again, it might not. You can move forward one small step at a time, feeling your way in the dark if you have to. All those small steps get you further than you think. Let love guide the way. Carve out that path with a (lovingly wielded) machete if you must. Douse the flames, the ones that are consuming you in ways that don't feel good, and lay a new spark in the hearth of your heart. Allow active love to transform your life for good.

Rewilding Spirituality

How does nature influence your spiritual life?

I grew up in the Evangelical Lutheran Church of America (ELCA), one of the more "progressive" denominations when it comes to protestant Christianity. We went to church most Sundays, and I can still hear my paternal grandmother saying grace before we dug into meals on the farm table, her voice rising for "Come Lord Jesus," emphasis on the first three words, and then dropping in tone a bit to finish with "be our guest and let these gifts to us be blessed." My maternal grandparents met working at a Lutheran Bible camp in Illinois. My parents met working at a Lutheran Bible camp in Colorado. My spouse and I met when on staff at a Lutheran Bible camp in Wisconsin. Lutheran Christianity will always be a part of my spiritual story for the simple fact that it's the first lens through which I consciously thought about God. I learned a lot about love, compassion, and empathy from the church and all those camps, and many communities of faith are doing good work in the world. Of course, organized religion has done its fair share of harm, too, from upholding systemic racism and the Doctrine of Discovery[1] (including playing a role in the boarding school system for Indigenous children) to encouraging homophobia to waging wars in the name of holiness. It's clearly not a sure path to peace. Religion is organized by humans, and humans are imperfect. Contained within the confines of religion is everything on the spectrum of what it means to be human, from life-giving to harmful. I suppose what I'm saying is that my faith and spirituality have been, and will forever be, an evolving story. If yours is too, well, welcome to the club.

These days I don't like to label myself as any particular brand of belief, though the teachings of Jesus certainly have a place in the evolution of my personal story of what it means to be a human being. I worked at four different wilderness-based ELCA youth camps during college and the years just after, and it's the fellowship, community, and proximity to nature that made me feel closer to a higher power. Ironically, it was my time completing a master's degree at a Lutheran seminary that I found myself becoming more welcoming of other belief systems. Less certain of my own. More inclined to ask questions and less inclined to say, "I know the answer." (Granted, it did take me three tries to pass the required Bible Proficiency Exam that was required for graduation—those ancient maps got me every time.) I found myself caring less about what happens *inside* a human-made sanctuary and caring more about what happens *outside* of the church's doors, amid the cycles of the earth. I wanted to spend less time dissecting scriptural texts written by men two thousand years ago and more time with the sacred that is nature itself. I wanted to spend more time outside in contemplation, in what my friend and writer L. M. Browning calls "wild silence."

A few years ago, thanks to (the positive aspects of) social media, I got to know Kevin Johnson. He's a writer, a self-described "recovering academic," and cohost of the *Encountering Silence* podcast, whose work is rooted in precisely what is being explored in this chapter: "rewilding" our spirituality—that is to say "restoring the bonds between nature, the wilderness, the body, the mind, and the soul." He writes, in an article for Patheos.com, "It is here, in the Silence, that prayer and contemplation connect. To know God, to know our faith, we turn to contemplation recognizing that it is a type of knowing that is much more immediate to life as it really is and not confined to words or ideas. It is a knowing through participation and encounter."[2]

If I had to make a broad claim about spirituality today, it would be that everything is connected—across borders and through space and time. The natural world is an essential part of the story. Encountering silence is as important as studying sacred texts (if not more so) in any relationship with the divine. Tradition, ritual, the land base, and daily living intertwine when it comes to cultivating a spiritual life, and all belief systems that nurture every form of life and accept all people with love have value. I believe that spirituality itself is a form of wildness. I'm with Mary Oliver when she says, "What I mean by spirituality is not theology, but attitude."[3] Perhaps finding that spirituality of wildness is tied to how we look at the world and how that worldview informs our attitude. Spirituality is a mysterious thing.

My family drove for seven hours straight west on I-90 every year, usually in summer, during my childhood. It didn't feel right if we didn't visit the Black Hills at least once a year. A drive around the wildlife loop in Custer State Park, heading to Crazy Horse Monument to check the carving progress, time spent on the shores of Sylvan Lake. (We always avoided Mount Rushmore and its blatant glorification of colonization.) And always, the journey to the top of Black Elk Peak. Back then, it was called Harney Peak, but the name was changed on August 11, 2016, a welcome shift for many. However, there are also those who wanted the name to revert to the original: *Hinŋháŋ Káǧa* (meaning "owl-maker" in Lakota). These sacred hills in South Dakota were taken from their original inhabitants, and we settlers often want to pat ourselves on the back for changing names of things to reflect our inclusiveness and commitment to diversity. How often do we get it right? Lakota folks should be able to name their own lands.

William S. Harney was a military man whose forces killed many Native American people in the 1855 Battle of Blue Water Creen (NE) and then led military expeditions through the Black Hills area in the 1870s. Black Elk was a Lakota medicine man who had a vision, at age nine while in a coma, that included the peak now named after him. He dictated this vision and many other stories to author John Neihardt after the two met in 1930, and the result of their talks is a book called *Black Elk Speaks*—the publication of which has resulted in the holy man becoming one of the most widely known Native Americans in the world. It's also gotten its fair share of criticism over the years for romanticizing the story into one of despair to having errors in translation to only focusing on the first twenty-five years of Black Elk's life (omitting the fact that he later became a practicing Catholic; he was christened with the name Nicholas in his forties).[4]

In the summer of 2018, we spent just a few days in the Hills, on our way home from visiting family in Colorado. We hit all the old spots: spent time in the company of bison on the wildlife loop, my daughter splashed in Sylvan Lake, and my spouse and I hiked to the top of Black Elk Peak. Some of the signs still say "Harney Peak," and some of the new signs that say "Black Elk Peak" have "Harney" carved into them in crude letters.

After three miles or so of mostly gradual upward walking, the path starts to get rocky, and switchbacks become the norm until you reach a bit of a clearing in the trees. Then the view opens up, allowing you to see for miles over rocky outcroppings that make up the landscape, always a landscape that has that blue/black tint in the distance. Then it's up some old stone steps, built in 1938 by the Civilian Conservation Corps when they replaced the old wooden fire tower built by settlers in the early 1900s. Though the stone fire tower was last staffed in the 1960s, it still stands and sees a great many hiking visitors during the summer months. But the stone fire tower isn't what claims my attention when I reach the summit. It's the prayer flags. There are a few old, gnarled cedar trees at the base of the stone building, and they are covered in Lakota prayer flags of all colors. Most of the hikers I see up at the top are tourists who are in the area for a short time, camping or re-creating (like me). Most don't pay the flags much mind, or if they do, they take photos of themselves in front of them. But when you close your eyes and tune out the noise and the selfies, you can feel the essence of Black Elk's vision rippling through time: "I was standing on the highest mountain of them all, and round about beneath me was the whole hoop of the world. And while I stood there I saw more than I can tell and I understood more than I saw; for I was seeing in a sacred manner the shapes of all things in the spirit, and the shape of all shapes as they must live together like one being."[5]

The flags rustle in the breeze, and just for a moment, when I look out over the jagged spires and into the distance beyond, I am encountering wild silence, the kind of silence that stretches out to connect all sacred things.

Thousands of miles from Black Elk Peak, on a rocky and wind-swept Mediterranean ridge, sits Ħaġar Qim. It is an ancient temple on the southern edge of the main island of Malta, one of five megalithic structures in the area, which are some of the oldest religious sites known in the world. I visited a few times when I was living on the island in 2001. The main temple is an arrangement of huge stone slabs, the largest standing sixteen feet tall and weighing twenty tons, and is thought to have been built between 3600 and 3200 BCE, a place for ritual and ceremony. One of the prehistoric chambers contains a hole carved out to align with the summer solstice. At sunrise on the first day of summer, sunlight passes through this hole to illuminate a stone slab in the interior. Today, the main ruins are under a large white tent for protection from the elements, but when I visited twenty-some years ago, they were still just perched on the hillside, out in the open. Nearby limestone cliffs jut out into a deep blue sea. I can remember walking up to the huge standing stones, worn down and rounded after so many years, marveling at how something can be so old and still standing, still projecting an energy that's just a little out of reach for a contemporary human (at least this one). There are whispers of something there in the silence between the stones. No prayer flags rustle in the salty air at Ħaġar Qim, but on the breeze there are hints of the rituals and ceremonies and contemplation that took place long ago.

Can the essence of Black Elk's vision be one that permeates time-lines and knows no borders? Nick Black Elk was a complex figure in history, and I wonder if there's something to be learned from that. And I wonder if the message that we, as a planetary collective, must find a way to live as if we are "one being" is more powerful than even an imperfectly complex (as we all are) messenger.

Years later, back home in Minnesota, I turned a rock, one with little holes punctuating its every curve, over in my hand, feeling the bumpy surface and rough grooves that being tossed around in the sea created. As I stood there in my basement with rock in hand as winter raged outside, I thought of the windswept Maltese beach where I picked it up, and a sense of connection washed over me. I thought of walking on hot sunbaked rocks along the Namekagon River in Wisconsin while leading campers on river trips. I thought of scrambling up scree fields en route to summits high in the Rocky Mountains. Touching bits of nature always transports me to places across the world, reminding me that, somehow, I am this rock, that beach, that dirt path even while I am this body, this mind, this spirit.

One deep winter day, on a walk around the woods by my house in piercingly cold (–10°F!) air, these words came to me:

Church of Shadow & Light

You know your holy places
by how accepting they are
of your whole personhood
by what you'll endure
to be there to pray

by the simple knowledge
that something shifts
each time you show up.

There is something sacred to be found in how the winter sun casts shadows on snow-covered ground or in how a walk through an old forest reminds you of what you are truly devoted to. There is something sacred in continuing to put your life energy where it is returned in kind. Somehow the wild silence ties all things together as one being, even when that silence also holds a continuing evolution of understanding.

Spirituality is an ongoing journey, and I can't claim to know the formula required to rewild it (since spirituality of anything is a pretty personal thing), but I do have a few strategies that have proven essential while on my own path. These are some of the notes to self from which I benefit by keeping close.

Go outside more than you think you should. Get intimate with what resides outside your front door, in the weedy patch between the two abandoned houses down the block, at the neighborhood park. Learn to love what's out there and let it love you back. Bring little bits of it inside. Keep going back out.

While you are out there, pay attention. Look up at the sky, breathe in the fresh air, feel the soil beneath your feet, notice the way the wind blows your hair away from your neck. Notice how the stuff of nature wants to interact with you and allow what you notice to influence how you are in the world. See if you can feel yourself as part of the wild silence. In the article I mentioned earlier, Kevin goes on to say that "we need to allow for more silent unknowing so we can work with how the mind naturally comes to know." Leave ample space for curiosity.

While you are paying attention and being curious, celebrate contrast. Diversity is essential for thriving life, and the wild is one of the best teachers of this truth. See the beauty in the garden as ten different types of vegetables and fruits and weeds all intermingle in a tangled mass. See beauty in how different your fellow humans are, those down the block and those on the other side of the world. Marvel at how good a warm fire feels after hiking in a snowstorm. Celebrate the fact that bright light makes shadows and the need for both to live into our creative human potential.

As you celebrate contrast and diversity, think specifically about your food. Even Jesus said something about the bread of life. Food is important when it comes to spiritual things. And when you eat a diet that is rich in color, texture, and varying tastes, you set your body up for optimal health. We need more than mono-cropped corn and soybeans to thrive. When we grow a wide variety of food ourselves or get it from others who do so sustainably, we play one small role in fostering better health for the earth.

Finally, while you are eating, let the food that you ingest remind you that you have a body and that your body works together with a mind and spirit, and those things are always trying to reclaim their wildness, both as individual entities and as members of a collective. As my friend Suzanne says, "Eating is a way to create a lived, embodied connection with those who came before us. To taste what they would have tasted and feel nourished in the ways they would have. See if you can work in your own ancestral foods, and as you're eating, bring that connection to mind. Feasting can be a shared experience across time."[6] The need for nourishment brings us together, over borders and across generations.

A rock and a memory, even on a snowy day deep in the winter of the American Midwest, has the power to remind me of the vast web that connects all things on the earth and my place in it. It reminds me of my own wildness and how essential it is to continue to claim it. Devotion to something starts with paying attention to it. It reminds me to pay attention to the bedrock beneath my feet and the sky above my head and the community, human and otherwise, in which I make my home. We are devoted to that to which we give attention. Let's give our attention to the wild, outside ourselves and within. As one of my favorite folk musical groups, Rising Appalachia, sings, "Dirt church is where I pray, you can find me there."[7] The lyric comes from a song called "Sassafras" on their album *Leylines*. The album title "alludes to the concept of invisible lines believed to stretch around the world between sacred spaces, bonded by a spiritual and magnetic presence." Leah Smith, a founder of the group along with her sister, Chloe, says their work has been to take the traditions (in their case, southern musical traditions) that they were born and raised within and rise out of them to create new bridges between cultures and stories, creating something new that's founded in heritage but is reflective of the current times. They are creating more pathways that bring us together as one being. That, to me, is the essence of rewilding spirituality.

Every time I've walked up a mountain trail, every time I stand in the midst of old stones by the sea, and every time I slow down enough to notice the way the wind rustles the trees in the forest, the piece of me that is akin to everything else in existence aligns with that "hoop of the world." I won't leave a prayer flag at the top of the Black Elk Peak next time I walk to the top, because that's not a cultural tradition that I can claim, but I will honor the prayers that are already there, those that find their way through timelines and across the sea, and those that are still to come. Each time I light a campfire, I connect with all the other humans who have done the same, in ritual or for simple survival, through the ages. We must walk together, as one being.

Paying Attention in a Digital Age

What truly sparks joy for you from the inside?

I remember what it was like to live in the analog world. I'm in what was one time referred to as a *micro-generation,* between Gen X and the Millennials, the one that included anybody born from about 1977 through 1983. As a kid, I listened to music on records and then cassette tapes. The rusty square-body truck in which I learned to drive a manual transmission had an eight-track player. It wasn't until my junior year in high school that my friend Jena helped me come up with my first email address. "Just use your first and middle initials with your last name," she said when I couldn't decide what to put in front of @hotmail.com. I took a class called Keyboarding, and the computers were huge machines that took up entire desks. We did research using encyclopedias, and there were limits to how many web resources you could use when writing a paper. I had a cell phone in college but almost never used it since it was so expensive (unless you waited until after 7:00 p.m., when minutes were free). I turned in my senior paper on paper, and it got returned marked up in red ink. Social media was not a thing until I was well out of college, though instant messaging had started to permeate the campus the last few years of my undergraduate days. Digital technology took on a life of its own at about the same time I did.

If you grew up in the 1980s or earlier, it's likely you spent much of your free time during childhood running around outside, making forts, chasing butterflies, or just kicking around with the neighborhood kids. Or doing chores, if you lived on a farm. You didn't have a cell phone, and the video game options were limited. Going outside was the best option, so that's what you did. (Or it's what your folks made you do.) According to ample research done since those days, going outside is essential for optimal cognitive and physical development. Children learn how to adapt to change, overcome challenges, and take healthy risks. They gain courage, build autonomy, and exercise creativity. They figure out what it means to be a part of a community that is bigger than what they can see on a screen and are more likely to develop a sense of responsibility to the earth itself due to being in direct relationship with the natural world. They intimately learn about the nature that is closest to home. They have the opportunity to love and appreciate and protect what they see as part of them.

There are a lot of things competing for our time and attention these days. In this technological age, it's important to spend time with the part of us that will always be a little bit wild. Like we discussed in the last chapter, it's what connects us to our fellow humans, across time and space and cultural divide. It's important to spend time with wildness, mind open to learning. Doing so invites us to listen and then use what we hear to work for good.

Somehow I made it well into the 2020s without a smartphone. I have a simple "call and text only" mobile phone (at least at the time of writing this), and it serves me fine. For years, my day-to-day work has required using a computer all day long, so the thought of spending even more time in front of a screen, no matter how tiny, is not appealing in the least. *However,* my spouse started using a smartphone several years ago, so now I use one of his old ones as a camera. It can't be used to make phone calls or text, but it does take photos, despite its cracked screen. If you are in range of a Wi-Fi connection, you can log into Facebook or Instagram or Twitter.

About 70 percent of the time, I find myself taking the iPhone with me when I go out, just to be able to snap a photo or two. It's nice to have some pictures of the parts of my life that happen outside of the living room—we live in an area with lots of lovely scenery. It's nice to have photos of my daughter as she grows. I have a slight obsession with taking pictures of plants, the garden, and food, so I have fun setting up shots in artful ways to capture the feeling of the moments and places that mean so much to me. These aren't inherently bad things. But taking pictures of them often quite effectively plucks me right out of the moment. As I try to capture it with a camera, I step outside of it, and its energy immediately changes. I'm no longer participating. I am capturing moments rather than being in relationship with them.

"Mom. Mom. Mom!"

I glance up, and my (then four-year-old) daughter is glaring at me from her spot in front of the woodstove.

"What do you need?" I ask her as I go back to pecking at the tiny keyboard of the iPhone, typing in a caption to go with the very artful and cute photo I'd just snapped of her.

"I want you to color pictures with me, not take pictures of me coloring."

Don't get me wrong: I love that I have all of these photos from the past few years of Eva creating art and playing outside and of the garden and people that I love. Photography is a fun hobby. I'd have far fewer photos had the iPhone not come along. Our other camera is a digital SLR, which takes great pictures but is big and bulky and not something that is easy to stick in my pocket on a hike.

One winter morning, after gliding across the ice-covered lake on skis, I turned east toward the rising sun and stopped in my tracks. It looked as though millions of tiny diamonds had been strewn across the surface of the frozen water in the form of snowflakes. I thought to myself that this must be what glitter is trying to emulate, like somehow stars have dropped out of the sky. The landscape hummed with the sort of shimmer only possible when light and snow are willing to fully harmonize. Had Marie Kondo appeared out of the ether to ask if it was a moment that "sparked joy," I would have said yes.

I stood there for a while just looking at the glittering landscape, feeling the sun through the chilly air, leaning on my ski poles. The iPhone with its camera had been left inside charging on the countertop in the kitchen. But I wished I had it. I wanted so badly to document the beauty I was seeing and share it with someone—and more often than not these days, that happens digitally, on social media. I'd rather say I just stood there marveling at nature's beauty, fully present and mindfully enjoying the view, but I'd be lying if I did. Instead, distraction from the allure of making an Instagram post out of what I was seeing dominated my mind. At that moment, I was trying to spark joy from the wrong place. Instead of living in the moment, I was imagining the next post.

It's a fine line to walk, isn't it? I need to stay mindful of some of the subtleties that drive why I take so many pictures in the first place and why I then so often share them on social media. On one level, I share all of these photos on various channels to keep my friends and family in the loop: My brother who lives in Colorado and my parents who live a five-hour drive away don't get to see our day to day as much as they or I would prefer. (During the quarantine days of the 2020/21 pandemic, this felt even more important.) I like spreading my love of growing vegetables and getting out into nature because I believe those things to be essential for well-being. You just never know when a nice photo will inspire someone to do something positive. Yet the energy of wanting more from a moment is hard to sidestep. I can't say I sidestepped it successfully that day out on the lake, but I am glad I noticed what was happening. Like we talked about in an earlier chapter, observing yourself doesn't always invite celebrational whoops. But the more I make a point to pay attention, the more I notice myself falling into the habits that don't serve the kind of life I want to be living. There is certainly a time and place for photography. Sharing photos is fun to do. (By now, we know that the dopamine hit your brain receives when people like your posts is fun too.) Thinking about how I'll turn a breathtakingly beautiful moment of stillness and light into a social media post is not how I want to move through life.

Where I run into trouble is when I can't remember how to spark joy without the share. I run into trouble when I can't remember how it feels to just experience something without making it into something else. I run into trouble when my memory of a moment is clouded by how other people responded to the fact that it happened. I run into trouble when my daughter can't get my attention because I'm looking at a screen.

Beauty should be shared—there's no question there. But beauty should also be experienced without turning it into something it's not. That day out on the lake wasn't an Instagram post. It was a human bearing witness to a brilliant tapestry of light, frozen water droplets, and air that will never weave together in that exact way again. A social media post can't capture that energy, no matter how expertly it is edited or how many little red hearts light up the screen after it's been shared.

Every couple of weeks when my daughter was a preschooler, we'd have what we called an "adventure day." We'd put on clothes suitable for the weather and head outside, usually to a local park or nature preserve but sometimes just down the path behind the house, always with the intent to explore. One late-spring morning, as we meandered through newly greened woods, stepping over old logs and around patches of unfurling ferns, we came upon a grove of lupines. Seeds from the neighbor's gardens had migrated over to this secluded patch of forgotten forest to claim the clearing we'd stumbled upon. There must have been at least thirty purple, blue, and pink flowers, some nearly four feet tall, offering us their jewel-like splendor. Exploring our immediate area resulted in discovering a treasure trove of late-spring wonder. Not having a picture-taking device in hand was the unexpected bonus—it offered an opportunity to be fully present.

I'm still working on my photo/presence balance, but it's getting better. Slightly. There have been a lot of relapses and chances to begin again.

The year Eva was in kindergarten, I got really sick, and our adventure days became fewer and further between. For nearly eight months, I struggled with a mysterious illness that persisted well after all the doctors I saw said, "You should start feeling better soon" while handing me their prescription recommendations and saying things like, "But you don't look sick." I still wonder where those three seasons went or where I was for them. Parts of me are still processing the anger and feelings of helplessness I experienced when I couldn't figure out how to get better physically. When the fog finally started to lift, it felt a little like waking up from a dream, the scary or depressing kind that you are ready to leave behind. The issues that came to light during my illness didn't just vanish, so even now I remain diligent about continuing to look at them: the need to be in control, to be viewed as competent and in the know, the constant push to do more and be more, the desire to prove my worth. It helps to have clarified the issues—to give voice to them. The exploration of what brings healing after a period of struggle can be a confusing time. My work is not done, but a bit more of a path has been cleared. Being present enough to notice wildflowers helps.

Heading outside the first few weeks I felt up for it again, after so many months of needing physical rest, served as a reminder that I am most content when in the here and now with myself, others, and the natural things of the world. Moving through a quiet forest, roaming with a child around a shimmering lake, following a deer path along a ridge, breathing in crisp, fresh air—these things are what feel real. It's not the photo I take or the likes that it gets on Instagram or the new followers that it entices to join my virtual following. (However, if you are part of my virtual following, I'm really glad you found your way to this book.) No, what matters is the actual experience. Perhaps this is obvious, but then again, it's easy to forget in this social-media-driven culture in which so many of us have become fully invested. I need to check myself regularly—it's all too easy to get sucked into the allure of virtual validation.

The basement is where the little router box that provides our Wi-Fi lives in our house. It's well out of sight. But, as it is in most modern spaces, the internet is pervasive. It seems to be able to find its way into every nook and cranny. It's alluring, and I don't like how it often dictates what I do and how I spend my time. Attention economy is a thing these days, you know. Our attention is a valuable commodity. (And that scrolling motion? That's actually addicting, kind of like a slot machine is addicting. It's that aspect of the unknown, the "what if I see something really great next? Just . . . a few . . . more . . . scrolls . . ." There are various delays and algorithms engineered into social media apps precisely to get a person to use the app for a longer period of time.)

As mentioned earlier, I am old enough to remember the days when the internet was still a destination, something you had to either go to (i.e., the library) or wait for (i.e., dial-up). It was annoying at the time, and having to do that now is almost unthinkable. (Unless you are a digital minimalist, which is also now a thing.) Despite the annoyance, that distance was somewhat freeing. There are countless memes that express sentiments like "offline is the new luxury," and perhaps that's the truth, at least for the average middle-class individual. The rise of internet technology has provided more opportunities for communication, the globalization of communities, and connection to more options than ever before. Those things offer a sense of freedom as well, of course: To do or connect with whatever you want. To organize grassroots movements. To bring folks together to do good in the world.

I heard author David Treuer speak about his book *The Heartbeat of Wounded Knee*[1] at a local bookstore just after it was published, and he mentioned that while many folks he knows living on reservations don't have computers, or even consistent living arrangements, they do have phones, and that has proven an important tool. Author Chris Stedman, in his book *IRL*, mentioned many ways that the internet has helped the LGBTQIA2+ community feel less isolated and more accepted. Phones have allowed many folks to continue to adapt and build resiliency while facing a culture that so often doesn't offer equality and respect. A culture that so often doesn't acknowledge that they are still very much a part of the collective story. The Black Lives Matter and Me Too movements gathered strength because of social media. People took to the streets in protest because of online communication. During the height of the COVID-19 pandemic, families said goodbye to loved ones via Zoom calls and livestreamed funerals. People gathered virtually to worship and celebrate when doing so in person wasn't a good option. Disconnecting isn't the best, or even a viable, option for many groups of folks. Being able to do so by choice is a function of privilege.

For those who have the choice, does the internet and our device use keep us, in a sense, captive to the quest to always be searching?

129

To "find our people" or our most well-suited hobbies or our dream vocation or the healthiest and most super of foods? That sort of "freedom" can prevent us from investing fully in what is right in front of our faces. What if we focused on getting what we needed, whether that be community or hobbies or jobs or entertainment or food, from within the twenty miles around our homes? What if we found community with the people who lived next door?

I find myself wondering if perhaps we humans aren't suited to existing in global communities. What if we really did keep the internet in the basement, only to take it out when it was truly needed as a tool or on special occasions for specific purposes? What if we only used smartphones for emergencies, like navigating an unfamiliar city at night? I remember that world, and even though my current employment and projects literally depend on easy access to the internet, I miss parts of it.

All of this is to say I have found that my health and well-being depend on fostering the right balance of analog and digital in this digital-focused world. Most of the literature I've read on how to live better with technology points toward the same basic principles. Perhaps you'll find these are things you know already too, deep in your bones: Be where you are. Develop the capacity to notice the details of the days. Reclaim your attention from that which wants to make it a commodity on the open market. Use new technology, but don't let it use you. Take time to explore what exists right outside the front door, from local flora and fauna to community to goods and services. Ensure your energy is being directed toward what is truly life-giving.

This is what I am going to do, and you can join me if you like: I'm going to see if I can experience more moments for just what they are, without making them into something else. Practice savoring the experiences that remind me what the texture of life can offer. Deny the pull to view life through an Instagram filter. Give more power to silence than the possibility of more notifications. Live in this moment, not the allure of what I want the moment to be. Use social media but not let it drive my choices or responses. I'm going to see if I can remember how to spark joy from the inside.

What does your life belong to? What *does* truly spark joy from the inside? These are questions we could all do well to ask on a regular basis. I will be asking myself over and over again because staying present and aware in the age of the internet, in the age of the attention economy, must be a daily practice. We must remember that true exploration takes investment in the here and now.

Declaring Your Place (in the Wild Family of Things)

What does it mean to you to be part of nature's family?

Some summer evenings, I go down to the lake and haul our huge green Old Town canoe over to the dock. I'm usually feeling determined to get a little time on the water after a long day of computer-based activities or schlepping around town. A canoe is not an easy object to lug around by yourself, but I manage to flip it over and drag it across the grass, onto the pavers-turned-dock-ramp, and then shove it off the dock into the reeds that line the shore. By the time I am situated with paddle in hand, fending off the spiders that always take up residence when the boat is not in use, I'm likely to be covered in dirt and more than a little annoyed at the heft of my chosen vessel. But off I go, paddling through the young lily pads—close to the edge first and then out into open water.

I'm fortunate to live next to this little body of aquatic life, yet so often I find myself feeling too busy with other things—work, writing, family obligations, dishes, keeping the garden alive, checking social media (wait, that shouldn't be on the list, should it?), and myriad other little details that make up a modern human life—that I don't get down to its shores as often as I imagined I would when we moved in. But I'm always glad when I do.

When the lake is calm, the fully clothed trees seem to preen and admire their reflection, flaunting their leafy abundance a second time over. As the sun sinks lower in the sky, the shoreline across the water blazes to life with the kind of light that can only last a moment, and then shadows move in swiftly. The flowers up in the garden wrap their petals around themselves, and the swiss chard stands at attention as the cooler evening air encourages better posture than the heat earlier in the day. On occasion, a floatplane buzzes by or a few cars, but most evenings a shroud of stillness overtakes the landscape. Cicadas hum, and frogs croak. The air seems to sigh and slide a hand down the curvy side of the hills. It's a sensuous world out there, and nature is the first in line to extend an invitation to dance.

One evening after I'd made it to the middle of the lake and beyond, I poked around near the opposite shore for a while as summer light invited the green of the trees to come alive with astonishing vibrancy even while the sun sank lower in the horizon. A great blue heron shared his space with me for a while, and we stared at each other until he decided to move his sentinel station elsewhere. Three deer silently watched me glide alongside the stately beaver lodge that sees new construction each year, unconcerned with my presence. Then one of the beavers slipped out, her coat silky with lake water as she swam around the tiny island near the northernmost shore, content to let me paddle along through the duckweed in her wake.

There are so many moments that make up a life. Many of these moments feel mundane, like a slow slog through a muddy swamp. Some are just plain hard and feel like running into a brick wall. But even during the slogs or the hard parts, there are bright spots, little shimmers of glitter. I like how Anna Quindlen put it in a tiny book titled *A Short Guide to a Happy Life*: "Life is made up of moments, small pieces of glittering mica in a long stretch of gray cement. It would be wonderful if they came to us unsummoned, but particularly in lives as busy as the ones most of us lead now, that won't happen. We have to teach ourselves how to live, really live . . . to love the journey, not the destination."[1]

Evenings outside allow me to focus on some of the small pieces of glittering mica. Even though some days seem more cement-heavy than would be ideal, the mica is still there. All I have to do is put a little effort into ensuring I continue to give myself opportunities to notice the glittery bits.

There is no arriving at a destination when it comes to living. There is only the journey and being present for it. Finding the small pieces of mica—from a canoe or from a city bus or while at the bedside of a loved one—matters.

It also helps when I recognize that my community is so much more than just other humans. During the winter of 2020, when gathering together with other people was on the "please don't" list, I found a renewed sense of community by focusing on the ground beneath my feet and incorporating it into my sense of belonging. I don't think I was alone in doing this. The lake out back, that winter, turned into a village green—even though we didn't usually spend our time outside in the close company of other people, someone plowed a walking path around the perimeter, two ice rinks were cleared, a cross-country ski trail ran alongside the walking path, and a few stick forts popped up along the shore. Folks I rarely see in the cold months, much less on the lake, regularly ventured out of doors and walked laps, claiming a place outside.

We may not have been gathering like we wanted to, but people find ways to cultivate community despite it all. Mary Oliver's "wild family of things" was there to hold us when we couldn't hold one another.

Summer evenings when I turn the canoe toward home, or in winter after a late-afternoon ski, I am greeted by a view of the sun sinking lower in the sky, clouds outlined by bright light. The reflection of the sky on glassy water or ice can only be described as otherworldly. But then again, there are other worlds all around us. We just have to pay attention and notice them. We just have to find the glittering mica in the gray cement. The sparkle in the swamp. The community under our feet when we thought we were alone. We just have to keep returning to that which lights us up from within. (Spark joy, remember?)

If there's enough light left when I'm done paddling, I often walk up to the garden. When it's blueberry season, I pluck the lingering berries one by one, occasionally slapping at a mosquito or waving away a deer fly. The tiny fruits, each one a deep indigo blue, fall into my hands, offering themselves for the taking. They seem to want to give themselves away, rewarding my desire for them. A stray blackberry bramble pricks my skin just enough to make me pause, and I notice the blue stains the berries have left in their wake on my fingers. I continue picking, lulled by the gentle drop of each berry into the container. When they take up as much space as I have to offer them, I make my way back to the house through the last bits of dusk. Grass tickles my ankles, and a low-hanging branch scratches the back of my neck as the house comes into view down the mossy hillside.

Placing the blueberries on the front step, I roll my shoulders back and look up, listening to the medley of life that has so graciously invited me in, giving thanks for this cool air, this gentle noise of night, this union with mystery, this time to weave my thread into this wild family.

Becoming Older (with Faith and Hope)

What does "collaborating with age" mean to you? How do faith and hope play a role?

Here are some things that remind me I'm getting older: My twentieth college reunion. Wrinkles on my forehead that are always there, even when I'm not trying to scrunch up my face. Realizing I've known my spouse for over 50 percent of my life. Being in a group at work for the "seasoned" employees who discuss things like rotary phones and tape decks. The desire to never wear uncomfortable clothes again because it's just not worth it. The absence of any desire to go out for the evening in any form other than to dinner or into the garden. And so on.

A few weeks before I turned forty, I had just started reading Parker Palmer's book *On the Brink of Everything: Grace, Gravity, and Getting Old*. I don't usually give much energy to contemplating my age, but that year aging and all that comes with it was on my mind. Early on, he writes, "How we travel the arc between our own sunrise and sundown is ours to choose: Will it be denial, defiance, or collaboration?"[1]

Obviously, at fortysomething, I am nowhere near being an elder in an era when people regularly live into their nineties. But something about entering into a new decade reminded me to be sure to collaborate with each passing year rather than trying to hold on to the things of youth that so often are sold to us as important or questioning the details of my life that are different from what we are taught to strive for.

I ended up having the day off of work on my actual birthday, and my daughter was at day camp, so I had some time alone. There are lots of things I could have chosen to do, I suppose. Shopping, getting a massage or a haircut, seeing a movie, meeting up with a friend, driving into the city to do something citylike . . . but what I chose to do was ride a bike down the road that we live on.

I didn't ride very fast, and I stopped a lot: once to let some geese and their goslings cross the road, once to say hi to a neighbor girl who was romping around in her yard, once to look at the reflection of some tamarack trees in the floating bog. Then I went over to one of my favorite trails, one that I usually run, and I walked slowly around a loop that's dotted with little streams and lots of ups and downs through the woods. Again, I stopped a lot: once to peer at a snail that was crossing the trail, once to look at another perched on a red-capped mushroom, once to wade for a while in the ice-cold creek. Nothing was accomplished other than noticing some details that I usually miss when I go by quickly in a car or running shoes.

Rather, I think what happened—in that act of pedaling slowly down a road close to home and meandering through the woods—is that I started to dabble in what it's like to collaborate with age instead of denying the fact that time is always passing. I wasn't defying the truth that slowing down is good (and necessary more than I think it is). I met the events of the day as they unfolded instead of always looking ahead to the next thing. We can't force ourselves to get older or stay younger; all we can do is let life take us where it will.

There are a lot of things these days that remind me that I'm getting older, inching closer to the "winter" of my life. But there are also a lot of things these days that invite celebration—celebration that becoming older is a gift, one that's worth the effort it takes to slow down and notice what is under the wrapping. If life is an arc between sunrise and sunset, embodying the speeds that allow us to savor the colors as they grow, evolve, and eventually fade is an essential part of the unfolding.

Winter—whether the literal cold-weather time of year, a fallow time in your life, or the last chapter in your life story—can be a hard season to be fully present. At the close of 2020, as the pandemic raged on and political unrest and white supremacy all seemed to be swirling out of control, the dark and cold days seemed like a low blow. How much can people endure? My household was struggling with everything from boredom to anxiety to social isolation to a deep need for solitude. News of another death, this time a writing colleague and mentor, crossed my desk the day after some hard conversations at home.

That evening, flames in the woodstove danced as the house settled and sighed in the early dark, and the first snow of the season fell outside. As the grandfather clock chimed the quarter hour, I closed my journal in frustration. Time continued to pass, and the flames continued to dance. I kept sighing deeply and eventually found myself turning to Mary Oliver's words, from her collection *Winter Hours*:

> In the winter I am writing about, there was much darkness. Darkness of nature, darkness of event, darkness of the spirit. The sprawling darkness of not knowing. We speak of the light of reason. I would speak here of the darkness of the world, and the light of___. But I don't know what to call it. Maybe hope. Maybe faith, but not a shaped faith—only, say, a gesture, or a continuum of gestures. But probably it is closer to hope, that is more active, and far messier than faith must be. Faith, as I imagine it, is tensile, and cool, and has no need of words. Hope, I know, is a fighter and a screamer.[2]

I reread that passage over and over again that winter, a winter that wasn't going the way I wanted it to go. It was like life was stuck but also speeding up and spiraling out of control. You've probably had winters like that too. Maybe the weather was challenging, or loved ones were struggling. Maybe losses kept piling up: layoffs, closures, deaths. Maybe you felt stuck in a job that you didn't like. Maybe you were in recovery or had just been diagnosed. Maybe you were just lost in that darkness of not knowing.

There at my spot by the woodstove, my frustration grew, despite my communion with Ms. Oliver's prose: I tried to pay attention to how it felt to write with a pen, to focus on the words in my book. I kept getting distracted by thoughts of tomorrow, bills that needed to be paid, the bits of wood that could be swept from the hearth. What would be coming next remained unknown, elusive as ever, and that was making me angry.

The flames continued to dance, but they were getting tired.

I wanted to stay inside that evening because who wouldn't on a cold, dark Minnesota night? But if I didn't go out, the fire would die. It needed more fuel, and that meant walking up the hill and trekking across the frozen field to the woodshed. Going out sounded like the last thing I wanted to do. Yet as I stepped into the frigid air, the night sky put out a welcome with the sort of twinkling you forget exists when you don't look up in the dark enough. A thousand stars blinked back at me, and the moon hung in the westerly sky like a painting of light, marking an ancient cycle. The cold cracked with the crispness reserved for temperatures most people don't welcome this early in the season, but on that night, there was something about the thinness of the air that felt necessary.

I walked to the shed, loaded up the wood carrier with logs, and made my way back across the frozen field, stopping twice to look up at those distant galactic neighbors. I felt my body tingle with the awareness that comes from knowing you are a small part of a universal whole, one that doesn't trouble itself with elusive things like worrying about errant wood chips or tomorrow's list. One that notices—and feels fully—the details, even if they aren't always comfortable. One that welcomes you into the cold, dark night.

In *Winter Hours*, Mary Oliver describes faith as tensile and cool, so maybe we say faith is capable of weathering tension and stress, the stoic presence that holds an unwavering strength in the simple act of being. Hope, faith's cousin, is the one who keeps the fire going. Fighting and screaming can take a lot of different forms, but regardless of the shape taken, hope is a tenacity for life. An unwillingness to let the embers turn to ash.

There are sixteen pages of prose between this first paragraph about faith and hope and the last sentence. They are all worth reading, but I'll just share the last sentence: "Weary and sleepy, winter slowly polishes the moon through the long nights, then recedes to the north, its body thinning and melting, like a bundle of old riddles left, one more year, unanswered."

That's the thing about faith and hope, isn't it? Getting to know them often leads to more questions than answers. But getting to know them also leads to being able to see the gleaming silver moon after a long winter of dark nights. Getting to know them, and allowing yourself enough of a pause, allows you to emerge from the deep freeze when the time is right.

Back inside, I put another log on the glowing embers, and the cats lay stretched as near the stove as possible. My daughter stirred, whimpering a story in sleep, and the neighbor's light shone brightly from across the lake and blinked out a few minutes later. The flames came back to life, taking up the dance again.

It's not always what I want to do, but to keep the flames alive, I keep going outside. Looking all the way up and rooting all the way down. No matter what the season, no matter how hard it gets. I do this to ensure I notice the way ice cracks in the sun. The burst of red when a cardinal visits the bird feeder. How cold air reminds me of how it feels to be alive, even when it isn't comfortable. I continue to build my capacity for attentiveness and accept that this doesn't mean knowing the answer. I practice being fully where I am and then give voice to the bits of astonishment that gather in the wake of doing so.

Will you try it? Get in on the conversation between faith and hope as you collaborate with age. Look up into a cold, starry night sky. Be attentive to the way winter polishes the moon and give in to wonder. Because the world needs us to keep wonder alive, no matter what season you're in.

Tapping into Tragic Optimism

What balance of growth and stillness serves you best right now?

I've been a runner for a long time. Most days you'll find me jogging a loop around the little lake in our neighborhood or out on one of the local trails. Three months into the pandemic in 2020, I realized that running—always outside—was one of the few things that was helping clear the fog of the times. At that time, the flowering trees were blooming at full force in my area, and they were spectacular. Their scent, as much as their beauty, filled me up as I ran. I didn't go far during those days. My usual loop was about two miles long. I wasn't training for anything. I've never been one to turn off the mind while running; rather, I tend to think more clearly about things that have been persistently shrouded in clouds.

Running, along with all of these flowering trees, helped me emerge from my pandemic fog. It also got me thinking about growth.

Our culture is pretty set on growth mindset or death as a way of operating. We hear from so many sources that we must always be looking for opportunities to grow, to strive, to put energy into personal development or furthering our careers in positive and visible and measurable ways. Shatter your glass ceiling, we say. Sky's the limit, we proclaim. Never give up, we advise. But what if letting something go, even letting something completely fade, is the best way forward? Where is the time for just living (and these days, for so many, just surviving)? Why is it so hard for us (and our employers or our loved ones) to let our roots tunnel deep down into the soil instead of focusing only on the blossoms at the end of the branches?

When my friend Holly was walking with her dad during the last part of his life, it was not a time of growth, in an upward and outward sense, for her. It was a time of bearing witness to decline. It was a time of slowing down, of listening, and of attending to this relationship that had been foundational her whole life. She wanted to turn inward and tend to her roots. Which is, of course, another way of growing, but it's not a way of growing that can be easily quantified and measured on a performance review or personal development worksheet. For her, it was a time of gathering the wisdom that comes from being fully present to the full cycle of human life. There are times during a human life when growth isn't, and shouldn't be, the priority.

The crab apple trees by my driveway always seem to flaunt their fuchsia, light-pink, and white blossoms. The flowers that have been tight little buds suddenly pop open and then reach their peak for a few days, maybe a week. Then the petals fall, and the trees' growth becomes more subtle. It gets harder to measure. Some trees do grow tiny apples, but all of the trees drop their leaves in the fall as they go into a time of dormancy. There is a short time for visible growth, and there is a time for gentle existence. There is also time to pause and let things go.

"Why have you been reading so much about death?" Julie, a long-time colleague of mine, tilted her head and waited for me to reply. We'd been sitting outside, idly chatting about the books we'd each recently read.

I looked out over the St. Croix River. The sun was going down, and I wasn't quite sure how to answer.

"Because I need to know it's possible to heal from the worst thing you can imagine happening and still be a whole person despite being shattered."

I'd read several books about death since losing a long-time job nearly five years earlier. That, coupled with a drawn-out illness, compelled me to search for something solid to grab on to amid the uncertainty of the uncontrollable. So death and dying seemed logical, I suppose. Death (in myriad forms) is one of the only certainties we have in this human life. Maybe immersing myself in stories about death and grief was a strange way to seek comfort, but those topics drew me in because I wanted to know people can go through heart-wrenching and hellish situations and live to tell the tale.

It was comforting to hear how a person's definition of "okay" can shift as an experience with loss is navigated and that the grief that accompanies a loss (no matter the circumstance) doesn't actually kill you, even if it seems like it will. It was even comforting to hear that if you are actively dying, there is still a sort of joy to be found in the process, as author Eva Saulitis wrote about on her CaringBridge blog three weeks before her death at the end of a long journey through breast cancer: "This is nothing like I thought it would be. This is more peaceful, more beautiful, more natural, more heartbreaking, at times more difficult, at times more easeful, than I imagined. The words pop up in my mind, and I hesitate to write them. I don't know if I'll feel this every moment, or if this feeling is fleeting like the last light in the sky."[1]

There is no comfort in denying the realities of a mortal life. There is freedom in opening to uncertainty, and there is ever-deepening mystery in accepting that loss and death are a part of a full life. The older I get, the more I learn—and the more I learn, the more I don't know. The more I don't know, the more I am convinced that embracing the unknowable is one of the places where true learning and wisdom arise.

There is comfort in knowing you aren't alone in the experience of loss, that it's a normal and necessary part of life, from a loved one's death to a cherished pet's to a job loss to species extinction to contemplating your own mortality. There is comfort in accepting that being okay doesn't look the same for everyone, nor should it. There is comfort in the belief that healing doesn't always mean finding a cure. There is comfort in allowing loss to be part of the fabric of a joyful life. There is comfort in taking the expectations you have about what joyful living should look like and laying them down to return to earth, the place we all return to someday.

Nearly everyone I interacted with in the thick of the pandemic was overwhelmed. Kelly felt stuck between work and homeschooling. Mara wasn't sure if she could support others in managing their stress because she felt stressed herself. Jamie, self-described as "super laidback and chill," kept finding himself short-tempered with his kids and husband. My colleague Julie described herself as being a "frozen frog" burrowed in the mud of a long winter, focused only on survival, unable to move forward, even months after things started to stabilize. The conditions created by the coronavirus pandemic didn't just go away, even while many folks strove to "get back to normal."

Tragic optimism, often described as the ability to maintain hope and find meaning in life despite its inescapable pain, loss, and suffering, is a term coined by Viktor Frankl, a Holocaust survivor and psychiatrist. Research shows that those who are able to tap into their tragic optimism cope better and can navigate challenges more effectively, even evolve in positive ways in the midst of hardship. I like to think of my crabapples as a very tragically optimistic variety of tree.

Even outside of the extremes of pandemic living, there tends to be too much work, not enough energy. Or there is no work and too many bills. Kids and employers and elderly parents require attention at the same time. People need more solitude and more connection simultaneously. So many folks are stretched in ways that make them feel like they are failing at everything. Call me idealistic, but periods of just doing what you need to do to keep your head above water don't seem like the best time to be striving for personal development. I'm inclined to suggest that during the hard times, we let the flowering trees do their thing, tap into our own tragic optimism, and let that be enough.

One late-autumn day toward the end of 2020, water droplets coated everything outside my house. During my walk around the perimeter of our hayfield, their tiny glistening bodies dripped steadily off the trees in the heavy air. Rain was never far off, and the view across the road into the fields beyond seemed out of focus in the foggy mist of a damp November day. Water pooled in the driveway ruts. It wasn't bitterly cold, but in that sort of late-autumn sogginess, a chill sticks to your bones with determination.

My community grieved that week after the loss of a devoted mother and spouse, a dear friend to many, a woman with a fierce commitment to her values. My own grandmother had died a few months before, and though it wasn't unexpected, there was a new empty space in my life where her physical energy used to be. A good friend said goodbye to her father after months and months of caregiving and, a few weeks later, her mother-in-law; then another friend died unexpectedly. She told me that she felt numb from all the losses that keep stacking up.

Loss, especially a physical death, feels shocking, even if you know it's coming. Especially if you don't. It takes your breath away. It can leave you feeling everything and nothing at the same time.

The news media has shared story after story about those who have died of COVID-19. That first pandemic year, college students gave up coming home for the holidays. More schools shut down in-person learning. More than one woman in my personal circle of friends gave notice at jobs they love to take care of things at home. Wildfires were still smoldering in the West after burning whole communities to the ground. Even minor calamities seemed more raw in a year filled with so many hard things, in an era when division seems to define too much of how we operate.

There were, and still are, puddles of loss everywhere. It's the one thing we all have in common, whether small (canceling holiday gatherings, not getting the haircut, accepting distance learning) or more significant (losing a job, a house, or a loved one). It can make everything else seem out of focus. It coats your bones with the heaviness of a steady rain. During those pandemic days, it felt constant.

Later in the afternoon, I opened the mailbox, hoping to find a few things I'd been waiting for, but all I fished out was a fundraising letter from *The Sun*. I almost threw it in the woodstove before opening it, but I didn't. Instead, I read what founder Sy Safransky had to say, and I'm glad I did because he closed his letter with this: "when the weight of the suffering in the world feels like too heavy a burden—this world that's so impossibly beautiful and unbelievably sad—I remember the advice of Edmond Burke. 'Never despair,' he said. 'But if you do, work on in despair.'"

The world may be both incredibly beautiful and terribly sad, but our work in it continues. In that work is the necessity to pause to be able to work another day. I can only hope that by fully grieving the unbelievably sad and allowing ourselves the stillness necessary to do so, we add another layer of depth to the impossibly beautiful.

If you need to press pause on striving—even if only in your mind—press pause. If you need help, reach out to someone you trust. Extend kindness to another. If you feel like crying when someone asks you how you plan to better yourself in the next three months, that's a sign that this is not a time to set lofty goals. A depleted being doesn't have the capacity to reach higher. This is a time to let the trees do the visible growing and nestle your roots deeper into the things that truly nourish you. Because you can't grow without nourishment, even if you want to.

There will be times in life that are not seasons of growth. That's okay. That's normal. Cultivate the conditions you need to navigate the season you're in. Remember that "thriving" can look different than the dominant cultural story wants you to believe. Be tragically optimistic during the hard times and hit pause when you need a break. Take your cue from the flowering trees the week after they drop their petals: you don't always have to be blooming.

An Invitation to Journey in Life-giving Ways

What does a good day look and feel like?

Open your eyes to the dawning of a new day and wander toward voices when you are ready for companionship. Embrace solitude if being alone fits right now.

Stretch your body, swim, canoe, run, hike, whittle, knit. Let your body move how it wants to move as light fills the sky. Remember that you are a body, and your body is you—you are partners in this life, not enemies.

Nourish yourself with seasonal food and fresh water. Enjoy coffee if coffee agrees with you and avoid it if it doesn't. Eat slowly and mindfully and welcome the energy of life-giving sustenance into your entire being.

Progress through the day with awareness and grace, whatever awareness and grace feel like to you right now. Don't hurry but move quickly if it feels good. Stop and rest when you need to be still. Do your work with the elegance of full presence and hold the space that wants to be held. Be sure to put it down when you get tired. Let others hold space for you too. Discern the difference between surrendering to what life wants and giving up.

Take in more nourishment when you feel hungry, be it food, rest, play, or prayer. Be reciprocal in your actions, always conscious of the give and take that creates the harmony needed to fill the hours with the music of beauty.

End the day with slow movement and breath and stillness. Quiet your mind. Sit in the peace that fills the spaces between your thoughts. Tap into the place of rootedness that is always there when you cultivate it.

Close your eyes to the gentle sounds of night inviting the day to fade and give thanks for another chance to rest and begin anew.

Part Three

Returning

re·turn·ing
rə ˈtərn/ing
come or go back to a place or person

Life on Planet Earth is a cycle, a continual returning—to the present, to what drives our actions, to the source that makes life possible. We are always returning, and even though there is no arriving at an end destination, we are always arriving somewhere. We're always arriving and always returning to the place that invites us to dance with mountains and look for the art in living attuned to our wild roots. It's a time for journeying forward, yes, but there is also a time for remembering and coming back. For using what we find in our origin and on our journeys as raw material necessary to fully become who we are and to integrate what we learn from exploring where we come from and what we learn from the journey through this life.

Accepting What Is

What do you need to accept to fully return to yourself?

When I go back to eastern South Dakota, the landscape where I spent most of my first eighteen years, I often run down to the river banks of the Big Sioux, my legs remembering the hundreds of other times I've run down this country road to start the day. Sometimes in the morning, the wind hasn't started blowing yet, and the sun glints off the still-dewy prairie grass and ditch sunflowers. Even though the view on this little jog has changed over the years—the gravel road now dead-ends at the river, the old bridge now years demolished; two new huge houses perch on either side of the family homestead; there are fences and new driveways where we used to roam free—despite these surface changes, the energy underneath, the whisper of the prairie as the world wakes up and the ancient undulation of the landscape, remains unchanged. It's always good to be there, in the place where I first grew roots.

This bit of prairie is where I go when I don't know what else to do, when I need to reset and regain my center. It's a place to be absorbed into land that taught me how to be alive, how to pay attention, how to see beauty in the ordinary, in the fleeting, in the fierce, in the unwanted, in the confusing, and in the humble. Somehow it's a place of enchantment, even as the trees I grew up with get bigger while others fall, as fences and houses go up where there used to be open space, as humanity moves over the land, oftentimes without compassion for what already lives in its path. Under all of that remains the hummus that continues to nourish my soul. The open space, the wide blue sky, the endless sea of subtle hills and grass—these things leave room for possibility.

My parents have both retired. Sometimes my mom talks about what they'll do next, where they'll live out their later years. I feel unmoored when I imagine the day when this house and this land are no longer something I can visit whenever I want to. I don't like to think about packing up the homestead, about other families living within those rough-hewn walls that my dad put up himself. Even though I don't make it back home more than a handful of times a year, this land formed me. But I can't claim it—it's no one person's, no one family's, to claim. I wonder (and need to continue to research) how to most effectively participate in the land back[1] movement if my brothers and I inherit this small parcel. Whatever comes to pass in the future, someday a different family will put down roots where parts of mine will always be, and theirs will join with mine and all of those who walked there before.

When I plant my feet in the soil, I feel the ancients rising and falling like the tides of old as a storm gathers strength. I feel the thin place where the reality that can be seen and touched exists right next to that place of the holy other, that place where, as Clarissa Pinkola Estés describes it in *Women Who Run with the Wolves*, "the dead come to be kissed and the living send their prayers."[2] It is a wildness, a recognition of something outside our understanding— something that is more vast than anything we can acknowledge with our human minds, our work deadlines, our politics, our finances, or our aspirations to matter. It's there to hold us even when we have to accept that returning to what once was is no longer an option.

When I stand on the hillside, the wind nearly always picks up, whipping tangled hair around my face. Ripples of rolling grassy waves seem to speak a language that I can almost understand if I allow myself to listen. It's a language older than time, and it tells the story of wonder. It tells the story of a beautiful sadness that I don't quite know how to look at. But I can feel it. The beauty is more powerful than the sorrow.

Later I rest in a field of big bluestem and match my heartbeat to that of ancient mountains and seas. Somehow I know the pulse of Gaia, of Mother Earth, parallels my own heartbeat. Like a drum beats, the pulse of the earth calls for deep listening and right action. It calls for acceptance of the unknown and fostering a love of that which we may never fully comprehend.

There are mountains here, in the deep, ancient energy that persists and invites tapping into the pulse. I can't see them, but I can feel them inviting me to dance. Maybe there are mountains where you are too, even if they aren't visible to the eye. Acceptance isn't an easy road to find. And returning to the parts of our origin, even if only in memory, even if all we want to do is forget, is to accept what remembering can offer. Then we can work on integrating the healing that comes from doing so.

Remembering What Was and Could Yet Be

What new pathways can remembering create in your life?

As a human collective, we're pretty good at forgetting. As Rabbi Rachel Timoner put it, when she was interviewed by Laura Esther Wolfson, in *The Sun,*

> forgetting is the single biggest obstacle to living the life we intend to live. Think about how we learn or improve ourselves: We observe our behavior and imagine a better way. We set an intention. We apply our will. But then time passes. We are busy. Our minds are pulled in a hundred different directions. We take the easiest and most familiar path. We forget our commitment. When we remember that we are not doing what we intended, we feel we have failed. If we dwell only on the

161

fact that we forgot, there will be no growth. But if we use that moment of remembering as an opportunity to return to our intention, we are one step closer to changing. We will forget again, of course, but then we will have another opportunity to remember and return.[1]

I, for one, am prone to forgetting all sorts of things. Where I put down my sunglasses. What we had for dinner last night. What my great-grandfather's name was. Where I come from. The hard history lessons that need to stay front of mind.

After all of my references to it, perhaps you've gleaned that I read *The Sun* every month. When I fish it out of the mailbox, there's a moment of glee when I think, *Yes! Something of value in the mailbox, finally.* I turn to the back page to read the quote page that they've dubbed "Sunbeams" to try to guess the theme of the issue. Then I see who the interview is with and usually start reading it while trying not to run into a tree on my way back to the house. This particular periodical has a way of reminding me what is important to keep thinking about. The stories shared in the pages aren't always easy to read. Some are full of despair and grief, but they always remind me to pay attention. They always remind me that forgetting is a daily challenge and that remembering must be a daily practice.

In my work as a wellness coach, I ask people over and over why they are trying to make changes, what they want to see for themselves, what is making now the time to focus on living differently. Most people come up with an answer pretty quickly—but the next week, maybe they slip back into old unwanted habits and beat themselves up over their perceived failures, or they lose focus and their commitment wavers, or life gets chaotic. The well-worn path is often the easiest route, even if it doesn't go where we want it to go. We forget where we're headed or why we want to get there in a new way. Often the forgetting is accidental, a product of simply having too much to do. However, sometimes it's intentional because looking at hard truths is, well, hard. And sometimes the forgetting is forced.

Hannah, whom you met in an earlier chapter, shared with me that her band of Mississaugii experienced extreme ethnocide through residential schools, boarding schools, government policies, and church. She explained that children on the reservation were targeted with the goal to "kill the Indian in the child." Women were subject to loss of "Indian status" if they married outside their own race. One of her aunts lost her status for a time because she married someone outside of their nation. Her grandmother's generation had culture stolen from underneath them. Only recently have members of her nation been able to start taking classes and learning about their heritage to regain that connection. To tap into that understanding of their ancestors. To relearn the language. To create their own regalia. To learn their stories, to revitalize their nation. To remember. Sometimes it's hard to go back. In the years I've known her, Hannah has inspired me to investigate more of my own cultural ties and ways my relatives interacted with the earth and the larger collective.

As Rabbi Timoner suggests, not all is lost when forgetting happens because each time we forget, we are offered another opportunity to remember. Each time we remember and act on that remembering, we create another path. Maybe it's not as well worn as the old rut, but it's a path that, with a bit of grace and grit mixed together, might just lead us through the forgotten pass (the one that's so often shrouded in mist or seemingly teaming with ferocious beasts) to what we thought was the unreachable far side of the mountain. Active remembering and reclaiming are part of what makes Hannah who she is.

The same is true for SunRose Iron Shell, a teacher and artist on the Rosebud Indian Reservation, which is just east of Pine Ridge in South Dakota. I first learned about her work after following the social media pages of a documentary called *Women of the White Buffalo*, in which SunRose is featured. During a live conversation about the film that I attended, producer Deborah Anderson spoke about needing the perspective of women, how their cultural roots are deep and ancestral ties strong. She said the film is about truth—and the truth is that women are still living these stories, right now today. She said that if we hold these stories in reverence, it'll help others do the same.

SunRose said, during the same conversation, that she often feels like she needs to "save the world." Since that's an overwhelming task for one person, she's focusing on what she can reach: her own family, her students, and her direct community. As a teacher, an activist, and an artist, SunRose is committed to helping her students tap into their Lakota roots. She says,

> My students have been told they don't exist; they are brainwashed into believing that they don't need to connect to their Lakota ways, their ceremony or language. When I first came to teach at St. Francis Indian school,[2] I was shocked to learn that most of my students don't even have their Indian names. Only a handful had gone to sweat. To the outside world they are seen

as unicorns, a rare breed, yet they have no idea. I feel it's my responsibility to impact them for the next seven generations through my art, through my passion to stay connected to our culture, so I can inspire these kids and bring them happiness and joy in remembering who they are.[3]

Each time a person, especially a young person, remembers who they are and acts on that remembering, another life-giving path is created.

About twenty miles south of my house is the farm site of Dream of Wild Health, one of the oldest and longest-operating Native-led and -focused nonprofits in the Minneapolis/St. Paul area. The organization was founded in 1986 by Peta Wakan Tipi to provide transitional housing and support services with a cultural focus for unhoused and chemically dependent Indigenous folks in the local area. The transitional housing program closed in 2011, but the farm is thriving on its acreage in Hugo, Minnesota. In March of 2020, they purchased an additional twenty acres within walking distance of the original ten-acre parcel. Executive director Neely Snyder told me, "This space will allow us to expand food production efforts and offer more space for our youth and community to gather, learn and grow." Today, the mission of the organization is to "restore health and well-being in the Native community by recovering knowledge of and access to healthy Indigenous foods, medicines and lifeways."[4]

From their youth programming to postsecondary scholarships for Native American kids to their Indigenous Food Network (*a collaborative effort to rebuild sovereign food systems within the inter-tribal Native communities*), Dream of Wild Health is committed to reclaiming health and vibrancy for future generations. More life-giving paths are being created through each seed they plant and each life that is touched as a result. Dreaming of wild health is something I think all human beings could benefit from doing in the ways that align with their deep cultural roots, and I'm grateful to this local organization for putting voice and action together to make that dream a reality for the community they serve.

I come from a family of farmers—from four generations ago in Norway and Germany to central South Dakota, where my uncles still cultivate the land my grandfather farmed. My folks taught us how to plant seeds, grow vegetables organically, and cook creatively (even though I didn't always appreciate those "creatively cooked" dishes as a youth). So I grow garlic, potatoes, carrots, kale, and tomatoes year after year, even when it's hard, like when bugs or small rodents or wild turkeys eat half the crop and I feel like throwing in the spade. I try to save some of my own seeds, swap with others when I can, and order the rest of what I need for a gardening season from Seed Savers Exchange.[5] We preserve as much of the harvest as we can, share what's in abundance, and eat together as a family. My dad's mom was a champion canner, and while I haven't mastered the art of pickling like she had, jars of pickles, tomatoes, and other preserves line our cabinet and freezer shelves every year. When the baseball-bat-sized zucchinis overtake the kitchen counters, my maternal grandma's zucchini bread recipe comes out. I freeze loaf after loaf to help sustain us in the winter months.

Just after we got married, Nick and I took a community education class and learned to make *lefse* from an elderly Swedish woman in an effort to claim part of our shared Scandinavian heritage. We got our own *lefse*-making supplies shortly after and have been making a big batch every year since, and our daughter has embraced the practice wholeheartedly. Nick's paternal grandmother's goulash recipe is in the regular winter dinner rotation. We get out the German advent calendar each Christmas and eat now and then at the local German restaurant. It feels important to stay connected to these things, even though traditional German food isn't my favorite. It's part of where I came from, and I want to remember that. I hope growing up with this closeness to where food comes from and the rituals of preparation and preservation help my daughter remember her roots and offer her a sense of belonging.

I also actively have to remember that as the descendant of settlers with European heritage, I'm a visitor on this land that we steward now in Minnesota, just as much as it's home. Much of what I have access to is because of generational wealth: the Homestead Act of 1862 granted my farming family access to colonized lands. I may always be unpacking and reconciling the complexities of this reality, yet I don't want to wait until I have it all figured out (I don't know if anybody truly gets it all figured out) to incorporate into everyday living this evolving understanding of what it means to be a good ancestor. As a coach, I am always telling people that I do not have their answers (as much as they sometimes want me to have them)—only they can truly figure out what the best course of action is. I don't hand coaching clients a tidy ten-step solution for healthy living because a shortcut to healthy living is not something that exists. It can take a good long while and lots of conversation to elicit the responses that lead to positive change. Even still, sometimes it *is* tough to remember that I don't need to have a resolution for everything immediately. When

I find myself wanting to be able to offer an immediate lesson from these stories of remembering and returning, I have to remember that I am not done learning myself. Therein lies the true beauty of coaching and, truly, of living in a supportive community—at its best, it can offer a space to simply *be* and the room to move forward when ready. I'm living a life that's still in progress. So are you and everybody else who's inhaling and exhaling throughout their days. And that's messy and nuanced and full of opportunities for mistakes and trying again, always returning to the new truths that are uncovered along the way and working them into the soil of our lives so they can provide the nourishment necessary to continue on.

One autumnal equinox evening, I went out to sit on the swing overlooking the garden. At 6:30 p.m., the sun was just starting to cast long shadows on the field, full of wilting and withering plants as cooler weather closed in. Cars zoomed by now and then, and the breeze rustled the aspens. The air was humming with cricket and birdsong, a timeless, age-old chorus of living sound. The apples were golden orbs in the late light, each one a tiny package of edible astonishment. Ripened fruit is dazzling in the way only ripening fruit can be, so I was glad I'd remembered to notice it; plenty of days I forget to be still and get sucked into the busyness of the day. That evening there was a stillness in the air, even as lawnmowers buzzed and people scurried about on their way home after a busy weekday. I was thankful to be there in the garden, witnessing the season shift, making a practice out of being dazzled. Making a practice out of remembering the part of myself that is part of earth's body, that needs wildness to thrive. I wondered who else might have been practicing the same, that very minute, across the globe. Surely there were plenty of others remembering.

REMEMBERING WHAT WAS AND COULD YET BE

Then the old orange rotary phone rang in the garage, and I thought for a second about going to check to see who was calling. There always seem to be many reasons to move when you are trying to be still. My attention drifted to a low growling coming from beyond the aspens where a motorcyclist was putting along well below their usual choice of speed on this road. I wondered why they were moving so slow. I thought maybe they, too, were making a practice of being dazzled in the fading light. There was bread (zucchini, of course) baking in the oven that evening, so I needed to go back to the house to take it out. Yet I found I wanted to linger, to simply watch the grass host these long shadows. To witness the flip, the turning of summer to fall. To be one small part of the great wheel, the one that will keep turning long after I am gone from this place. I wanted to meld the moment to memory, to invite it to be part of me, just like I was part of it.

As I practice remembering, I often discover that taking the well-worn path is less appealing after I've seen what that far side of the mountain can offer, whether the far side showed me the beauty in moving slower than usual, in asking hard questions, or in looking closely at something I'd rather forget. Maybe you will find some valuable insights on the far side too. We won't get there all at once. Perhaps we'll only visit the far side now and then. That's okay—it's just a matter of continuing to visit until the far side isn't so foreboding anymore. Once we learn what has come before us and the other stories that make up the history of the land, or the origin of our heritage, we can't go back. We can forget or look away, sure. That happens all the time. Yet we can also remember. Actively remembering helps harness some of the power necessary for living the life that is ours. If remembering is available to us in a way that does us no harm, it's another way we can contribute to the healing of the world. Each time we do it, we've reinforced our foundation and created another life-giving channel.

Every time a person remembers what they need to remember in order to connect with an essential piece of themselves, it's another wisp of hope rising.

Seeing Wisps beyond the Horizon

What else is possible?

I read once about a small shorebird, the *Calidris canutus rufa*—commonly known as the red knot. Writer Deborah Cramer penned a number of essays, published in *Orion Magazine*'s spring 2020 issue, that accompany paintings of the birds done by artist Janet Essley. These little birds, just the size of a robin, make one of the longest journeys on the planet, from South America to the Arctic and back again in their yearly migration. Along the way, they sustain themselves with horseshoe crabs in Delaware and mud snails in Brazil. A nesting period in the Arctic results in newly hatched young feasting on insects during the Arctic summer. Climate change and human activity are disrupting the patterns these birds know deep in their DNA, but nonetheless, they persist.

The stories Cramer shares in her essays, about the red knots, are an eerie read during this time on earth—this time when humans are being impacted by a global pandemic, when systems cease to function for myriad reasons, when refugees flee war-torn lands just to be turned away or jailed where they thought they might be safe, when creatures of all sorts disappear every day. We are living in a time of deep transition, even as the economy grinds to a slow crawl as people grapple with how to live during a time of uncertainty.

"The juveniles . . . somehow make their way unaccompanied . . . finding a route they'd never traveled, heading toward a place they'd never been."[1]

Cramer is talking here of the red knots who hatch in the Arctic and find their way to a home they've not yet seen but somehow know deep in their bodies. When the time comes to migrate, they stop to feast on clams in James Bay, Ontario, and then fly on, nonstop, to South America.

They haven't ever been where they are going, much like we humans haven't been where we are going, either. I think we know that things can't go back to business as usual—somehow we know that's not where we can stay.

One of the essays is about how the birds have been hunted widely over the years in some places, from Cape Cod to Guyana. (International coalitions are currently working on preservation efforts.) Cramer writes, "I see a sadness in Essley's painting—birds in disarray, scattered, a trail of blood encircling the flock."

It seems like there has been a collective sadness hovering over much of the planet for a while now, but it was heightened in 2020 and again in 2021, and yet again in 2022. On a video call with my family during the early days of the COVID-19 pandemic, one of my brothers spoke of some colleagues who weren't able to see their parents before they died because if they went to say goodbye, they'd be exposed to the virus. Around the same time, a friend who's already survived a civil war and periods of time as a refugee expressed heightened anxiety and depression, made worse by feeling trapped at home. Countless young people in high school and college were not able to walk across the stage in celebration, weddings were being postponed, family reunions canceled. So many were out of work. BIPOC individuals and groups continued to be disproportionately targeted, incarcerated, and killed by law enforcement. George Floyd, a Black man, was killed by (now former) police in broad daylight on a Minneapolis street, and the glow of flames from the uprising and protests the weekend afterward could be seen from well outside the city limits. The very old couldn't keep company with the very young for months. Hundreds of thousands died. As vaccines were developed and policies about safety measures like masks and social distancing shifted, many communities splintered as these things became politicized. Indigenous folks and their water-protecting allies continued to stand against Line 3 in northern Minnesota (a pipeline constructed by Enbridge Energy, a Canadian company, that violates treaty rights of Anishinaabe people and other nations in its path) and were arrested, shot with rubber bullets, and tear gassed, including during ceremonial prayers. The Russian military invaded Ukraine and millions of people fled the country within weeks. There was, and still is, a lot to grieve, no matter how you have been impacted by what's happened on the world stage.

Cramer goes on to say, "And yet, in the painting's beauty, vibrant color, and potential flight of a bird . . . there is hope."

There is hope, of the active sort, being practiced all over the world. Of course, there are those who are in despair because there are places where things are very bleak. It's incredibly challenging to navigate continual loss, whether it's a physical loss of life, employment, or physical safety to perceived loss in the form of deep uncertainty. But despite the very real hardships, there are many doing the work of buoying spirits, of holding space, of healing, of offering aid when aid is needed.

In the final essay in the series, the one about the red knots returning home to southern Chile, Cramer writes, "Each day birds come in with the tide, first appearing as tiny wisps of distant smoke, and then as giant clouds sailing over a tidal plan for miles wide, stretching all the way to the horizon."

The place in Minneapolis where George Floyd was killed, even though the intersection was reopened after a full year of being blocked off to car traffic, is a memorial where people come together to grieve and acknowledge the deep pain of injustice that has been a reality for African Americans for over four hundred years. In early 2021, youth from the Standing Rock Indian Reservation ran ninety-three miles to pressure President Joe Biden to put a stop to the Dakota Access Pipeline for good. Women continue to advocate for fair treatment and equal pay in the workplace. Dr. Rachel Levine became the first openly transgender person to be confirmed by the Senate as the assistant secretary to the US Department of Health and Human Services. The California-based Evangelical Lutheran Church in America

(ELCA) Sierra Pacific Synod elected Rev. Megan Rohrer as its first openly transgender bishop. Deb Haaland, member of the Pueblo of Laguna and a thirty-fifth-generation New Mexican, became the first Native American individual to serve as US Secretary of the Interior. Each of these is a wisp of hope, rising.

Despite the hardships that have befallen so many all across the world in recent years, there is beauty being uncovered: from how folks are stepping up and speaking out to help one another to the way migratory birds continue finding their way home again.

Anxiety and despair and anger are all very real. So is beauty. There is loss and anger and uncertainty swirling around us all. Yet there is also a tiny corner of peace, or maybe you could call it possibility, in each moment, like a wisp of distant smoke. Things will continue to shift, they may well get harder before they get easier, and conditions on the other side may be different than we are ready for. But just like a juvenile red knot, we can learn to listen and find our way home again, even though the terrain of the future is unknown.

Beautiful and terrible things happen every day, and it's always been that way. Fear and anxiety are normal, and you are allowed to feel what you are feeling—but you don't have to let fear drive. Feel it and then turn to your support network, get some fresh air, and pay attention to the things in your immediate physical space. Claim who you are. Accept. Remember. Nourish your roots and look all the way up. Keep your eyes on the distant wisps of smoke. There may well be a giant cloud of hope stretching toward the horizon if we have the patience to watch for it.

When options feel limited, sometimes it's the simplest questions that illuminate the path forward—and it's not always the path we think of when we consider what's next. Could you allow for a new possibility, one that perhaps you've not yet considered?

What else is possible?

Activating Hope through Grief and Gratitude

*What happens when you let grief **and** gratitude have the space they need?*

Do you ever feel like if you were to fully consider everything you could think of that's wrong in the world, you'd have no time or energy left for anything else? Many of the words that describe what's happening on Planet Earth right now don't make a person want to jump for joy or sigh in relief. The Amazon burns, while floods swallow sea-level neighborhoods. Planned power outages become business as usual to prevent wildfire, while incredible amounts of energy are used to keep indoor ski resorts going in deserts. People in high office in too many countries seem to have missed the history lessons about the horrors that result from unchecked, systematic racism and the dangers in acting from fear and entitlement. Constant economic growth remains the goal, while finite resources vanish. Work hours are long, jobs are lost, people are sick, loved ones are hurting, the dog is getting old.

There are many things to lament and grieve. There is, of course, goodness and that which is worthy of gratitude alongside the parts that make you want to scream in frustration or shake someone. Yet sometimes (oftentimes) it's hard to notice the good stuff. Grief and lament have their place in the world, and they are necessary. Grief is a form of love. So is giving thanks. Gratitude is nearly always possible, even in the midst of grief.

As I mull what I've just written, I find myself drawn by the words of Holocaust survivor Elie Wiesel. He said, "When a person doesn't have gratitude, something is missing in his or her humanity. A person can almost be defined by his or her attitude toward gratitude."[1]

It can be tempting in the face of loss to look for silver linings or to say, "Just focus on what you still have." But as Megan Devine, author of *It's Okay That You're Not Okay,*[2] says, "Gratitude is not the Tylenol of life." Practicing gratitude doesn't change what's wrong. Practicing gratitude doesn't mean burying unwanted feelings or looking for the silver lining in a bad situation—it means acknowledging what is still good alongside the mess. You can experience grief, or anger, or overwhelm even while you are grateful for the good things that remain.

Beth came into our coaching relationship as a former heart disease patient, just looking to keep up the healthy habits that she'd put into practice after a cardiac surgery. With a clean bill of health and the okay from her cardiologist to visit him annually for a checkup, her goals stemmed from the desire to support her husband in eating healthier so they would both be able to fully enjoy their retirement years. She embraced gardening, got really creative with whipping up interesting dishes from quinoa and millet, and loved to share her new finds with me in the realm of healthy eating. Over the years, she had ups and downs with meeting her goals, but she always showed up to her appointments, her commitment to support her husband never wavered, and she always wanted to continue to push herself to be able to retire into good health as her last day of work approached.

Then one day I called for our scheduled appointment, and when she answered the phone, I knew something was different. Her voice was flat. When I asked if our appointment time would still work, she said yes and burst into tears.

After a few moments, she was able to explain what was going on, and I learned that her beloved husband, the man she raved about on every single call, to whom she was extremely devoted, had died unexpectedly in an accident. Her hopes and dreams for retirement had been turned upside down. She felt like the rug had been pulled out from beneath her. And indeed it had—life as she had known it would never be the same.

We got through that call, and she left with some goals to explore the grief counseling available to her through the funeral home and make sure to eat at least one full meal every day. I felt a little unsure about how to proceed as her grief and sadness were so very raw. Beth continued to show up to our monthly appointments, and she started grief counseling. She also joined a support group, which eventually turned out to be a very good thing, despite the challenges she had with opening up for the first several months. She gradually started eating more again and making healthier meals, though she continued to struggle with gathering up the motivation to cook for one. She made goals around inviting people over and getting out into the community. At each meeting, we talked about her husband, what she loved about him, and how much she missed him. She continued to cry every time we spoke. At one point in the midst of all of this, I took what felt like a bit of a risk and brought up the concept of a gratitude journal—not really knowing how it would go over but feeling like it might be okay timing now that she'd had several months of grief support and had been open to exploring more new things during our last few sessions. She agreed to give it a go and write down three things each day that she was grateful for, no matter how tiny, at the end of her day.

As humans, we are prone to feeling all sorts of things. Though I'd rather not put people into categories and boxes, people tend to understand the language of a label. In keeping with that philosophy, a label that we need to use more is *grieving*. By *grieving*, I don't mean sad, or feeling sorry for ourselves, or giving up. I mean seeing what is going on in the world and loving the world anyway: loving what is passing away and seeing things to their end; feeling the enormity of what has happened or is happening and not looking the other way.

In October of 2016, the Great Barrier Reef off the coast of Australia, the world's largest and most diverse place of aquatic life, was declared dead by *Outside* magazine. (Shortly after the piece was published, it was shared that 22 percent of the coral is dead, or bleached out, not to be confused with the entire reef. But still.) The people of island nations continued to struggle to rebuild that which was just barely standing after yet another disaster hit their shores. In 2020, Australian bushfires ravaged the country like never before, and at the very end of 2021, the most destructive fire in terms of structures lost burned through a heavily populated area in Boulder County,

Colorado. In early 2022, eastern Australia was impacted by severe and historic flooding. Whole species of animals and plants are dying out at alarming rates, and we're in what many environmentalists call the "sixth mass extinction," an extinction event caused by human activity. Violence remains a normality in too many parts of the world. Distraction wins more often than not, unless you are right there in the thick of the issue. Then survival is all that matters.

Around the same time that the *Outside* magazine piece came out, I read a book about a man's journey to walk the Nile in Africa.[3] The author, Levison Wood, spends time in Rwanda, and he said that despite the strides that have been made the last twenty years in the effort for reconciliation, it feels like a haunted place. The genocide that happened there in 1994 is not easily forgotten, nor should it be. It's something to be grieved. (This is easy for me to say from across the world. Could I say it as a Hutu or a Tutsi? I don't know.) But perhaps the feeling of haunting that Wood experienced comes from the struggle of a nation to truly feel their pain and come to terms with what happened—with the blood that seeped like water back into their home soil. Perhaps some of it comes from grief. Mr. Wood said that some of the people he met in Rwanda were actively trying to forget. We do what we need to do to cope.

I don't think we need more guilt, or rage, or powerlessness. We surely don't need more entitlement, self-hatred, or shame. But we do need to grieve that which has been lost, that which has died, that which we or our children will never have, and that which is at this very moment fading away. Stephen Jenkinson says, "Grief requires us to know the time we are in. We don't require hope to proceed. We require grief to proceed."[4] Taking a cue from Sufi teachings and the concept of oneness, we are all part of the same whole, and this includes the earth as much as it includes other human beings. Witnessing the destruction of creatures, parts of the planet, and parts of the self is cause for grief.

I appreciate Joanna Macy's description of how hope can look, that if we take an active stance, it "doesn't require our optimism, and we can apply it even in areas where we feel hopeless." She writes that "the guiding impetus is intention; we choose what we aim to bring about, act for, or express. Rather than weighing our chances and proceeding only when we feel hopeful, we focus on our intention and let it be our guide."[5]

Almost ten months after starting it, Beth was still keeping her gratitude journal. There had been a noticeable shift in her energy a few months into the practice. We continued to talk about her husband, but there was an incredible sense of joy mixed in with the grief that will always be with her. She spoke of how grateful she is to have had him in her life and how much she is still learning from him as she goes through his office and books and personal items that she wasn't able to touch before. She shared she was going to the opera weekly, taking yoga and Pilates classes at the gym, and that her next goal was to visit the botanical gardens that surround the cemetery at least once a month to walk mindfully in nature. She was studying things like neurobiology and attending lectures at the local university, and she was excited about getting back into her garden to start growing herbs again for her cooking experiments. She was able to fully experience grief by exploring gratitude alongside it, and it propelled her to activate her hope for the future. She acknowledged the difficulty of loss and grieving but didn't rush it. Beth uncovered the good that was still there in the midst of those hard things.

We need to acknowledge the time we are in. It's a downright terrifying and ugly time for way too many forms of life. It a hard time for the Great Barrier Reef and the land of the Bakken Oil fields and the war-torn streets of Syria and folks with brown skin, people born into poverty, and individuals who are gay, transgender, or nonbinary. It's a hard time for anyone who has experienced loss, and in the aftermath of the pandemic, that could describe nearly everyone alive. If the world were a house, there would be rooms for gratitude and joy and celebration, but there would also be a room that can only be filled with grief. The house will feel empty until the grief is acknowledged, and the door into hope will be stuck. I don't know about you, but I'd like the doorway to hope to be open fully for all.

At the end of the day, we need to acknowledge our grief and, when we are ready, channel it into active hope. We need to bear witness to what is going on, even on the toughest of days, and in doing so acknowledge and honor the deep parts of what being human on this earth is all about.

We don't need more angry, hardened hearts. We don't need more despair. We need more hearts that have broken open so wide that they can contain infinite love. We need more hearts that listen to the cry of the other and the cry of the earth. We need more hearts that allow gratitude to sit next to all the other things that need attention. Not gratitude on demand—gratitude as foundation. We need more hearts that beat in harmony with ancient rhythms that persist despite the frustrations of the times.

When I can remember that my heart pulses with the same energy that flows through the veins of the land, the rivers; when I can remember that my home is on sacred ground, Mother Earth; when I can see my own humanity reflected in the eyes of someone with very different views than my own; and when I can remember that the squirrels and fox and deer with whom I share space are my kin, I can let my heart break open to feel some of grief that the world needs to feel to invite wholeness and healing. I can go directly to the source of what makes life possible.

Going Back to the Source

*What does "going back to the source"
mean to you?*

I walk through the tall grass toward the place where the water bubbles out of the ground, cold as ice and clear as fresh air. To get here, you have to drive down a winding back road and pull off to the side of it to park and then hike down a steep trail that, until a few years ago, was unmarked. Or, if you start from the official trailhead, the way to get here is via the most remote trail, the one that goes all the way to the edge of the park boundary and connects with the next less formal trail system beyond. There is not much human foot traffic here during the week—in all the times I've visited, I hardly ever see another person. Usually it's just me, the birds, an occasional fox, and the deer who silently watch from their posts in the forest. Going all the way to the source is perhaps not the most popular choice.

There's a silica sand mine, a place where parts of the earth are extracted for use by humans, just up the banks of the St. Croix River, near the little town of Osceola. It's about five miles from where I am now as the crow flies. Friends who live across the street from the mine speak of early-morning truck traffic, shaking ground, new sand at the bottom of their well, and new worries that life as they know it may be forever changed if proposed expansion is allowed to continue unchecked. I don't live close enough to the mine for its existence to impact my day-to-day life, but I, too, worry.

In these parts, most hikers choose a route along the rocky outcroppings and sheer bluffs along the St. Croix River at the parks that maintain trails—and for good reason. They are breathtakingly beautiful, dotted with towering white pines and mossy boulders left here and there from ancient glacial activity. The mighty river itself has a strong pull. You can feel its power when you draw near. After all, it has carved a vein into the earth. But today I'm not by the river. Today I'm stepping over the marshy places in the ground and over rotting logs, and eventually I come to this place where something new begins.

As I walk, I worry about how the mine expansion could impact these waters, already threatened. I worry how the marshy places and the mossy boulders and the rotting logs might suffer as more and more is taken. I worry about what will happen if we don't take time to truly listen for what the best way forward is for all beings. I worry that good intentions to honor mining permits aren't enough. I worry about what it means when business owners have more rights than ecosystems.

I stand at the edge of the small pool surrounded by stones, watching. As the water bubbles up from the earth, the sand at the bottom of the pool continually dances and resettles in a rhythm that doesn't cease. It is the definition of persistent. Being in the presence of this subtle energy reminds me that there are things in nature ensuring the mainstream isn't the only stream. The river is fed by this gentle bubbling that meanders downward over rocks and roots until it joins the larger body of water. It is fed by something that is easy to forget about and sometimes hard to reach. But when I can remember that this gentle energy is what feeds the larger river, and that all of the other little tributaries in the watershed do the same, I am reminded that these tributaries have influence that can be tough to see. The impact, though subtle, is there.

But I worry that gentleness, this subtle energy, will be snuffed out by the constant need for economic growth. I worry that bubbling springs and dancing sands will be eventually replaced by mines that want this sand to make things that people use and eventually discard. I worry that my definition of persistence isn't enough.

This mighty river commands attention and has the power to carve veins into the land. So do the bubbling springs and the tiny tributaries. Every time one of those little streams carries something important, the mainstream is impacted, for better or for worse. It reminds me that it's important to stay true to my own voice, even if it's not loud or it goes against the grain. Making a point to keep the tributaries clean and clear matters in profound ways, even if we can't see it right away. Even if it's hard to do.

I want my young daughter to be able to stand at the edge of this spring, or on the banks of the river, and marvel like I do. I want her to know a world that includes mighty rivers and dancing sands and migratory birds and fish who need clean water. I want her to be able to go to the source. I want to live in a community that honors these things. I want to live in a community that partners with the ecosystem rather than one that lords over it.

Take a moment and consider the largest river in your general area. Where does it start? What feeds it? If there aren't many rivers close by, think about another natural feature, like a grove of aspen, a tract of tallgrass prairie, or a pine forest. A great lake, a wild rice bed, or a cypress swamp. How do you feel when you're close to these bits of wildness? When you think about them? What needs to happen to keep them healthy, especially if they've been negatively impacted by human activity? Imagine what it would be like to live in a world where nature had the same rights as humans. A world where going back to the source and ensuring it has what it needs to thrive is part of the story of the people. We humans, especially those of us with privilege, are going to have to give some things up and live differently.

Wild rice (*manoomin* in Ojibwe) has sustained many generations of Anishinaabe people, and it needs clean water to thrive. In 2018, the White Earth Band of Ojibwe in Minnesota formally recognized the rights of this important part of their culture. Three years later, in 2021, the tribe sued the Minnesota Department of Natural Resources in tribal court on behalf of wild rice, arguing that a water use permit that was issued for the Enbridge Energy Line 3 pipeline (that was under construction and nearing completion that summer) puts wild rice at risk. It's one of the first cases of its kind to be brought before a tribal court, part of a growing movement to establish legal rights for nature instead of treating it as property. Hannah, my coaching colleague who you met in an earlier chapter, spoke about this one day during a chat. "Manoomin is sacred in our culture. It is a part of our prophecies. It guided us in our travels and helped us know when to stop moving. As an Anishinaabe whose nation lost our manoomin's ability to grow due to environmental racism, Line 3 represents harm to Ojibwe people and harm to the manoomin's right to flourish. And once lost, you are always acutely aware of what was stolen when visiting the water."

We must ensure this vital source of life, water, is protected. It's a source that supports all of life on earth, and it's one we need to return to again and again, even if only in memory or hopefulness.

I kneel down by the spring to feel the cold, clear water. As I do, through the ripples I catch a glimpse of what can happen if we go back to the source. I catch a glimpse of the more beautiful world that is possible when all perspectives are considered.

Harmonizing through Generations

How are your threads woven together with the threads of others?

The *nyckelharpa* showed up on our doorstep in February in a huge box packed with more crumpled newspaper than I've ever seen in one place. My spouse unboxed the traditional Swedish instrument, examining it for damage from its journey from the Ohio-based craftsman to our house in Minnesota. After declaring it unharmed, he tuned it per the instructions that came in the box. Then he plucked one of the strings and tried to figure out how to hold it properly. Three days later, he could play a few simple songs. Every time he does, the resonant sound of Scandinavian music fills the whole house, six hundred years of this type of instrument's musical history vibrating through the strings.

Like me, Nick has quite a bit of Scandinavian heritage. Some of his ancestors emigrated to the Upper Peninsula of Michigan from

Sweden, and his paternal great-grandparents eventually settled near Duluth, Minnesota. I've always liked folk music, but ever since our daughter was born, we've found ourselves drawn to *Scandinavian* folk music. Even when she was tiny, Eva loved listening to the contemporary Finnish band, Frigg, and she started pretending to play a fiddle when she was just a year old. Now she and her dad are several years into fiddle lessons with a local teacher, and I like to think of it as a way that she's connecting to her cultural heritage. Does she always want to go to lessons or practice? No. But she and Nick are creating a connection to one another and their shared cultural roots by taking these lessons together.

In addition to an assortment of fiddles of all sizes, there have been two jewelry boxes in my daughter's room as she grows up: one new, bedazzled and pink, a gift from her aunt; and one old, weathered, and wooden, a box that had been my maternal grandmother's. When she lifted the latch on the wooden box for the first time, at age five, Eva looked up at me wide-eyed. "It's like beautiful treasure, Mom." She promptly clipped on a pair of old pearl earrings, fastened a delicate watch around her tiny wrist, and lined up the rest of the box's contents in a row: a garnet and ivory brooch, some old buttons, a long silver chain, a white pendant with gold accents, three pairs of emerald-colored earrings, and countless singles that had lost their partners over the years. Once everything was out on the floor or draped over her body, she looked at the empty box with satisfaction and closed the lid.

After years of living on her own after my grandfather died in the 1990s, the combination of age, decreasing mobility, and memory issues prompted a move for my grandmother from her home state of Indiana to an assisted living facility where my folks live in South Dakota. Grandma was still Grandma, my mom's mom, but she wasn't able to put memories together like she wanted to and was getting confused more and more easily. She wanted to talk about Borchers, her old German church in southern Indiana. She stashed chocolates in her dresser drawers. She got concerned when she called her little brother on the phone and he didn't pick up. During one of my visits, she told me a detailed story about being the only girl on the county's softball team in the 1940s—she played first base, and her team was good. Eva got called my name most of the time. Grandma often asked when it was going to be time to go home, though she eventually stopped trying to leave the building on her own. Her memories came and went and got mixed up. Some were gone, some returned in unexpected moments of clarity, and others left for a while, just to come back when she was trying to remember something else. But her story persisted, even under layers of forgetting.

It was shortly after she was moved into memory care that I found that old wooden jewelry box among her things during a visit. All the stuff that didn't fit in Grandma's new room got stacked in my parents' garage. When I opened the lid of the box, there was a handwritten note tucked inside, nestled in with the dangly earrings, gemstone bracelets, and brooches—a note to my grandmother from my grandfather, who had died twenty years earlier. The paper was yellowed and looked like it came from a notebook. The words, over seventy years old, were cursive, in faded black ink. The simple sentiment said, "To my dearest wife: Occasionally through history a man is privileged to have a wife who is special above most other people—kind, understanding, gentle, with a quality born of an inner sense of goodness. I know this isn't a great big gift—money couldn't buy a gift big enough to express my feelings for you. Thanks for being who you are. I love you."

I sank down on the garage floor between some old throw pillows, a box of china, and the deep freeze and slipped into another time. It was a glimpse into the intimate history of my family—a place that feels almost too close to the bone but an important place to be for a little while. Almost an invasion of privacy, but in a family that doesn't always talk about feelings, one I was grateful for as a way of seeing into what it was like to be my grandparents, all those years ago. Somehow it mattered to me that the note was a physical thing—a yellowing piece of paper that was touched again and again—instead of a digital record that can only be viewed on a screen. My grandmother saved that note for decades. I can only guess how she felt when she received it, but I am willing to bet that she felt seen and loved.

Eight months into the 2020 pandemic, Grandma had a stroke. We hadn't been able to see her for months, other than a masked and distanced visit with my folks in the courtyard on her ninety-third birthday.

I got a text from my mom a few days after getting the initial call. "She hasn't eaten. She can't swallow so she's not drinking either." A few hours later, my phone pinged again. "We called hospice." We packed up and set out on the daylong drive to South Dakota.

As I walked into her room at the care center, one of the nurses was just leaving. Grandma was slumped over in her recliner, eyes half closed, right side of her face sagging in unfamiliar ways. "Hearing is the last sense to go. She knows you're here. You can talk to her."

As *A League of Their Own* played on the TV, I thought of her stories about playing first base. I told her about what's going on at our church and with Eva's violin lessons. I flipped through a copy of *Better Homes and Gardens* and pointed out some lilies that looked like the ones I'd dug up from her yard years ago when she moved into her first assisted living apartment. Unable to really communicate or move, she cried now and then. So did I.

At the end of my last visit to her room, as the aides were bustling around, I rubbed her thin shoulder through her nightgown. Perched on the edge of a straight-backed chair, I felt awkward in my mask and unsure how to say goodbye. I leaned over and said, "Thanks for being who you are. I love you." She couldn't respond in a way that I could understand, but I hope she felt seen. That she mattered to me and always will.

Grandma's old wooden jewelry box is still in Eva's room years after we first brought it home. When I look inside, I find the old costume jewelry, earrings, the watch, the chain, the pendant. The brooch and some of the earrings are missing, and the chain is broken. There's also a Barbie shoe, four marbles, a piece of driftwood from Lake Michigan, a bit of moss from the yard, lipstick, an old cell phone, and a glittery blue pen. As Grandma's memories shifted and faded, these reminders, these little physical pieces of her story, have been gradually woven into Eva's as she's been creating her own. What it was like to be Grandma and what it's like to be Eva have some commonalities now, even if some of them are just little bits of jewelry and the creak of an old hinge. It's been a way for them to communicate without words, or even presence, through the tangible. Eva and my grandmother will never spend an entire weekend together making cookies and reading books; they won't exchange letters; they won't have a full conversation on the phone. But opening that wooden jewelry box, selecting a necklace to wear, and fastening the clasp—even some seventy years apart—is a representation of what binds them together.

As the years progress, more genetic similarities between Eva and Grandma will surely show themselves, from facial features to personality traits to the grit that develops over a lifetime—because these two stories, one that is just starting and one that has completed the final chapter, remain forever intertwined, no matter what a human mind forgets or what objects are lost or broken or kept forever. Even if that old wooden jewelry box turns up empty one of these years, the story will remain very much alive in the empty space that is left behind.

The week of her death, I set Grandma's paper weight, the one that always sat on her desk, on my dining room table. Its deep blue flowers, flecks of green, and the elegant way it casts light around the room remind me of her. Her lilies and succulents are planted in my garden, and her old wooden jewelry box continues to invite Eva into imaginary play and cradles a love of treasures old and new, tangible and abstract. Grandma knew exactly where Malta was, including the type of landscape I could expect to encounter for my college semester abroad, when most others had never even heard of the tiny country. She wrote countless letters, maintaining communication with everyone from friends of distant relatives in Germany to her wayfaring grandchildren. She loved chocolates and planting flowers and the exploration of far-off lands. She grew up on a small farm in southern Indiana, and I can imagine her running barefoot across the newly greened grass on a morning in late spring to collect the eggs from the henhouse or simply to feel the bright air on her skin. Grandma's mother, my great-grandmother Lillian, adored flowers and planted row upon row of cutting flowers by the farmhouse. She nurtured perennials, fruit trees, berries, and persimmons and knew the land could support her family's survival if she took care of it. This love of rolling hills, streams, plants, and beauty runs through my veins, the veins in my own mother, and those in my child. It's a story that persists. It's one of the threads that weaves the family together.

To be part of the fabric of a family is to be one thread in the weaving together of stories: some happy, some sad, some full of grief, some full of joy, some annoying, some endearing, some that will be easy to forget, and some that are burned into memory forever, even if memory eventually starts to fade. It is being in relationship with others, even when there are no shared genetics, or when the family unit is a mixture of the unexpected, or when the threads start to fray at the edges.

A collective, a unit of individuals who are together, either by choice or not: that is what makes up the fabric of family. When it is at its most beautiful, that fabric illustrates the witnessing of life through a lens of compassion. It is allowing love to be the garment we wear every single day, no matter how hard the circumstances. It is journeying alongside others using the threads of compromise and integrity to be sewn together in ways that prove durable enough for everyday living.

When it's warm, sometimes Eva will take her fiddle outside and play it in the garden or while she's walking through the grass near the hayfield. Those days, when simple music finds the summer air, it's like, as Rumi said, stepping outside the circle of time and inside the circle of love. Love for earth, love for sky. Love for those who came before and those who are yet to be born.

At the end of the summer in 2021, Nick had the opportunity to save a classic 1958 wooden boat from being destroyed if he went to pick it up from the guy who wanted it gone. The catch was that it was a few states away in Indianapolis. Since school wasn't in session yet, he asked Eva if she wanted to go along. She did. She wanted to visit her great-grandparents' graves and spend some time in the state where they lived most of their lives (just like she'd visited her other great-grandparents' graves in Minnesota and South Dakota). At age nine, she knew that returning to part of her origin story was important to do. So they went, and she collected another piece of her history as they drove under the August sun and by endless fields of corn as Indiana cicadas hummed in the distance, welcoming them in and then sending them home again.

I found a folded-up piece of paper in the old wooden jewelry box one day not long ago, as I was helping Eva look for something. This one I left unread. It's part of her becoming, perhaps to be discovered by another pair of hands someday in the far-off future. It's one more thread in the story. It's one more way to harmonize through generations.

Becoming Earth

What changes when you declare going outside to be as essential as breathing?

I am becoming earth. I run through an old-growth forest on the heels of a wolf, dive naked into a cool pool of water, soar with the cranes over the plain, and howl at the full moon while dancing under shimmering stars. I sleep outside in the elements and use mud as sunscreen. My hair is tangled and full of leaves and small sticks, and I drink sunlight and bathe in the power of the moon. The earth is my mother, and the sky is her lover. I am married to myth, and my children are whispers of ideas that float on the clouds. Dirt and ferns and vines creep around my body, and I can talk to the trees in a language older than time.

The alarm clock goes off, and I wake up. I'm wearing navy-blue pajamas. As I rub my eyes, I realize I spent the night sleeping in a bed next to my spouse. There's a meeting on my calendar in twenty minutes, and I can't remember how to talk to the trees. The dream slips away like sand through an hourglass.

I want the earth back.

As the day progresses, I notice the birds calling to each other and feel the breeze caressing my bare shoulders as it rushes through the open windows. A few hours later, I step away from the computer and out of my shoes onto the lawn, touch the rough bark of the huge silver maple in the yard, and I remember that becoming earth isn't out of reach, after all.

Becoming earth means lifting my eyes to the sun that peeks through the clouds on a dreary day during a slow walk through a park. It means stepping outside under a sliver of a new moon and wondering where the light has gone through fears that just won't stop. It means putting my high heels in the closet for good because they just aren't worth it. It means being an advocate for those forms of life who don't communicate in ways that technology and progress can understand. It means listening to the stories of those whose voices have been, as Arundhati Roy said, "deliberately silenced or preferably unheard."[1] It means looking into shadows and dreams and stuff that no one wants to talk about because it isn't pretty or nice or put together. It means a lot of things if we let it.

It means being fully alive while I draw breath.

In her book on creativity, called *What We Ache For*, Oriah Mountain Dreamer says we need to "find the marriage of meaning and matter in life and in the world." That's what we ache for, isn't it? To touch and truly know the "fire of being fully alive."[2] Being fully alive seems to be the ultimate goal, even though it can be hard to express what that means or looks like.

What is "being fully alive"?

Some days, being fully alive is noticing the way the sun casts dappled light and shadow through still-bare tree branches. It's watching that light stream through the window, making dancing shapes on the table and on part of my left hand. Other days, it's sitting in a rocking chair, air dry and warm by the woodstove, listening to a fire crackling as early-arrival sandhill cranes and geese trill and honk overhead as they make their way back home again in spring. It's noticing the smell of woodsmoke that lingers when I step outside and the sound of the seasonal stream trickling in the ravine by the south side of the house. It's witnessing vibrant green moss peeking out from the patches of snow that persist and the tiny water droplets that hang on newly unfurled spores. Being still enough to notice these things, these ordinary details, is what makes me fully alive.

Sometimes, though, it's moving quickly on foot or bike that does it, the rush of wind on my face a reminder of aliveness. Sometimes it's the giggle or earnest comment from my child—the marvel of her existence and evolution into her own personhood a continual astonishment. Sometimes it's picking a ripe tomato or digging through wet soil until I find a treasure trove of purple potatoes. Sometimes it's the buzz of deer flies as I try to stay one step ahead of them on the trail. Sometimes it's air that feels too hot or too cold or the way spongy moss claims the shadowy parts of the yard.

It all comes back to the noticing—to actively rejecting the pull to numb the unwanted. To be willing to open up to the wonder of walking through a forest at dawn, fog rising from the lake, day stretching out like a canvas waiting for the combination of noticings that will transform it from blank slate to something lovingly and curiously created from the raw stuff of living.

Carin lives in a northern region of Sweden, a region ripe with opportunities to walk through forests toward misty lakes at dawn. As is so often the case in this digital era, we met on social media. Several years ago, one of my books crossed her path, and she let me know the material resonated by way of a few comments and direct messages on Instagram. We've been following each other ever since. Her feed is full of ambient photographs of nature, illustrating how a human can melt into the landscape and how noticing the details can add another layer of beauty to an ordinary day. When I asked her why nature connection is important in her life, she told me that the forests and meadows of her home country have always spoken to her, that she feels like she belongs to those pieces of nature. Her heart is filled with love for wildness and for her ancestors who lived there before her time. She works with young children at a kindergarten and considers showing them the blessings nature can offer in their lives to be her most important task. Nature is her soft place, and connecting her human life to the wild parts of herself and the world fills her with hope. Without connection to the earth, she would lose her way. This bond with the earth, who she lovingly calls Gaia, makes her world sane. Connecting with earth makes her feel fully alive and has been essential to her becoming. When I see her photographs, often images of her or another human standing in a foggy meadow or by an old gnarled tree, I'm reminded that humans and earth are not separate beings—we are part of the same body.

Becoming earth means leaning into that which is wild, true to nature, and authentic to what it means to be a human creature. It means embracing the wild self in all the ways it wants to show up. The wildness that can be found in all of us can be subtle, but it is as opulent as it is gentle and as quiet as it is screaming from the tree-tops. It is all that we can imagine and all those things that we still cannot. It is the ordinary days and the terrible days mixed with the magic of life on a living, breathing planet. It is walking through an unknown door toward something that has burned up to see what wants to rise from the ashes. We become earth when we can recognize ourselves in the reflection of whatever adds healing to the world. We become earth when we remember what we knew before we were born, when we tunnel our roots down deep, and when we listen for the voices in the stones.

An Invitation to Keep Going Outside

What does going outside offer to you?

Go out into the woods, child, go out. Let your feet carry you on the worn path behind the house, down to the marshy shores of the lake.

Go out into the woods, child, go out. Wander into dense tree cover, trail your hand over the bark of an adolescent maple, and find your shelter among roots and branches.

Go out into the woods, child, go out. Splash through the puddles that pool at the base of the valley and listen to the call of the sandhill crane as it soars over dying autumn crops.

Go out into the woods, child, go out. Lie down in a grassy field and let your gaze drift with passing clouds as leaves rustle their lullabies.

Go out into the woods, child, go out. Race through blazing midday light. Once you are tired, pick up a stone and let your hand fit its shape to the smooth sun-warmed surface.

Go out into the woods, child, go out. Rest in the shade of an old oak tree and feel the wisdom and strength of deep roots and patience fill you up with something you didn't know was missing.

Go out into the woods, child, go out. When the time comes, let the earth gently cradle you as your body returns to the shadow of the mountain.

Go out into the woods, child. Go out.

Parting Words

How can you add healing to the world?

Eva Saulitis wrote, in her final collection of essays, *Becoming Earth*, "I died and you died and the ever-moving earth continued on and on. There is a future, and it is not us. It is the mountain. It is the earth."[1] At the end of the day, living well is not just about our personal journey—it's about living in such a way that we honor the life that's going on all around us. Especially for those of us who can be called settlers, it's about decentering ourselves and getting out of the way to follow when it's someone else's turn to lead. It's about doing the work we need to do to add healing to the world.

You and I, our neighbors and those in far-off lands, animals and plants, atmosphere and bedrock, the threads that weave us together as one body—all of this is earth and sky colliding in a dance of mystery. On some level, our ancestors knew this, even if we have to dig back a thousand years to uncover the relatives who were truly attuned to the earth's rhythms. We need to acknowledge where we come from, journey as we're called to, and integrate what we learn so our descendants get the chance to experience being fully alive on a vibrant planet. The trees need our songs of lament and promise. The soil craves the replenishment we are able to give. The stones want us to listen closer. We do not need to know all the answers, but we need to listen and be open to what we hear. Nature is an essential partner in the dance of living.

To dance with mountains—to become earth—to harmonize through generations is something done every time we draw breath, from the first to the last. After the final breath fades away like the whisper of a dream, still earth and sky collide.

Acknowledgments

So many individuals and groups have offered support, conversation, and simple presence in the process of writing this book. It's a journey that I could not have embarked on nor completed alone, and I'm so thankful for all the helping hands I've encountered along the way.

I am deeply grateful for the encouragement and guidance of my editor, Lisa Kloskin, copy editor Rachel Reyes, and the rest of the team at Broadleaf Books: Thank you for helping midwife this book into the world. I so appreciated the chance to learn alongside you as we navigated the editing process with the additional support of Salt & Sage Books.

Thank you, Melody Bates, Chris Burkhouse, Holly Walsh, Taryn Montgomery, Kifah Abdi, and Rebecca Long, for all the conversations about books and about what it means to be a good human. Hannah McCalip, I am so thankful for your work in sharing information about all the different perspectives of Indigenous folks from around the globe and for building a workplace community devoted to all things Indigenous.

ACKNOWLEDGMENTS

Thank you, Hannah McCalip, Juliana Aragon Fatula, Aimée Medina Carr, Rowan Lischerelli, Christina Beck, Stacy Bare, Christina Ettestad, Carin Collin, and Chrystal Odin, for answering my questions and allowing me to share parts of your stories. Your willingness to share your perspective gave this book so much more depth. Thank you to Neely Snyder at Dream of Wild Health and SunRose Iron Shell, for granting me permission to share your perspectives.

Thank you, Ellie Roscher, for your continued encouragement and support—as well as for writing your next book at the same time as me. It was strange to not have you in my Google Drive for this project, but knowing you were writing at the same time kept me going.

Thank you to my Simple Collective colleagues—your support within the realm of social media buoyed my spirits when I felt like disconnecting for good.

I'm grateful for the community and daily support in my coaching world—thank you, Maryn Fulton, Tiffany Jansen, Megan Norwalk, Julie Wild, and Grace Spratt, as well as Brooke Marchand and members of NKOTB (you know who you are).

Thank you, Bayo Akomolafe, for showing me that dancing with mountains is a viable option that's worth putting energy toward. Thanks, Alissa Wild and Kevin Park—I still credit my time working on We Are Wildness projects years ago as one of the things that truly opened the door to exploring the concept of wildness. Thanks to all the writers who have shared their stories in books and interviews and newsletters, whose work has been important in the evolution of my own understanding of the world, and of whom there are far too many to list but especially Chris La Tray, Kaitlin B. Curtice, David

Treuer, Anton Treuer, Diane Wilson, Robin Wall Kimmerer, Austin Channing Brown, Layla Saad, Ijeoma Oluo, Lyla June Johnson, Quinn Gathercole, L. M. Browning, Brene Brown, Charles Eisenstein, Stephen Jenkinson, Theodore Richards, Kevin Johnson, Wendell Berry, and Kent Nerburn.

Thank you, Nick, for reminding me to go outside when I don't feel good; thank you, Mom and Dad, for taking me into the woods as a child; and thank you, Eva, for reminding me to look at things with curiosity and ask questions.

Last but not least, thank you to all of those with whom I have shared space: in the garden, on the trail, in a canoe, in my memory, and as a memory someday in the future. You are all a part of this story. And of course, thank you to Mother Earth for making stories about collisions of sky and earth and dancing with mountains possible in the first place.

Appendix
Digging Deeper into Self-Inquiry

Land Acknowledgment/Preface/Introduction

What does your own land acknowledgment say, and what actions will follow it?

When have you gone "there and back again" in your life?

Would you rather reflect on questions to identify your own way forward or be handed a solution? What makes you feel that way?

What invitations do you notice in your own life?

Origin

What comes up for you when you think about where you come from?

Which land base, culture, ceremonies, rituals, or groups are part of your origin story?

What matters about the beginning of your story?

How does origin intersect with belonging for you?

What about nature reminds you to remember your roots?

Are there parts of your origin that trouble you or that you'd rather not look at? What would happen if you did?

What makes you feel connected to the core of who you are?

What's the story of the land where you live now?

What do you hear when you listen to the history of the land?

What character traits of your own can you celebrate?

What aspects of your being do you need to more fully claim?

How does the nature/earth connection help you do your work in the world?

What have you witnessed that needs to be shared?

Journey

How do you get started with something new?

What part of a trip away from home do you tend to enjoy the most? Why?

Do you feel lost in any aspects of life? How come?

What have you learned from periods of time when you didn't know where to go next? What gets most of your attention right now?

Where do you need to bring your attention more often?

What does being mindful mean to you today?

How would you describe your relationship with nature? How about with technology?

What's the best balance of analog and digital for you these days?

What senses or sensory activities help you experience a sense of belonging where you are?

What would it be like to take up space in a way that feels right and good?

What relationships are important on this leg of your journey?

What do you need to nurture to grow in a life-giving way?

In which aspects of life do you need to allow yourself to pause and rest? What would be the benefits of doing so?

What part of the day do you tend to enjoy most? What makes it enjoyable?

Returning

How do/could you integrate what you learn on your travels into everyday life?

How does acceptance show up in your life?

What do you need to accept right now?

What do you need to let go of?

In what aspects of your life do you feel most rooted?

What do you love about the world? Why do you love it?

What would you rather not think about? What would happen if you did?

What land base do you long to return to? What makes you long for it?

What organizations are doing important and life-giving work in your area? How could you contribute or get involved?

Where do you see hope rising?

How do grief and gratitude fit together for you?

What do you need to grieve?

What's the difference between sadness and grieving for you?

How does it feel to acknowledge that death is a part of life?

How does time spent outside help you?

How does the concept of family play into your personal story of
  returning to your roots?

What forces are colliding in your life right now?

What would it be like to dance with mountains?

Notes

A Land Acknowledgment

1 To learn more about how to develop your own action plan to support Indigenous folks, visit https://nativegov.org/beyond-land-acknowledgment-a-guide, a guide developed by the Native Governance Center based in St. Paul, Minnesota.

Epigraph

1 Kent Nerburn, *Native Echoes: Listening to the Spirit of the Land* (Saint Louis Park, MN: Wolf nor Dog Books, 2017).

The Invitation to Dance with Mountains

1 Many of the ideas in this section came into being via dialogues in a course facilitated by Bayo Akomolafe called *We Will Dance with Mountains: Writing as an Ally for Emergence.*

Part One

1   Aimée Medina Carr, *River of Love* (Pawcatuck, CT: Homebound Publications, 2019).

Digging for the Truth

1   Nick Estes, Melanie Yazzie, and Jennifer Denetdale, *Red Nation Rising* (Oakland: PM Press, 2021).

2   Wendell Berry, "A Native Hill," in *The Art of the Commonplace: The Agrarian Essays of Wendell Berry*, ed. Norman Wirzba (New York: Counterpoint, 2003).

3   Thunder Valley CDC is committed to "Living Lakota liberation." Learn more about its work at https://www.thundervalley.org.

4   As Nikki Blak pointed out in an Instagram post on December 27, 2021, "Just because you're [I'm] experiencing discomfort does not mean you [I] are [am] being harmed."

5   Juliana has published two books of poetry: *Red Canyon Falling on Churches* and *Crazy Chicana in Catholic City*. Learn more at https://manyblankets.wordpress.com.

6   Kent Nerburn, *Native Echoes: Listening to the Spirit of the Land* (Saint Louis Park, MN: Wolf nor Dog Books, 2017).

7   Robin Wall Kimmerer, ed., "An Offering," in *Braiding Sweetgrass: Indigenous Wisdom, Scientific Knowledge, and the Teachings of Plants* (Minneapolis: Milkweed Editions, 2013).

Listening to the Land

1   Learn more about the Gammelgården Museum at https://gammelgarden museum.org.

2   Learn more via the Friends of the Karl Oskar House at https://www. facebook.com/LindHistSoc.

3   This river was known as **Hogan-wanke-kin** to Dakota people. The contemporary name, St. Croix, came from French-Canadian fur traders, who saw a huge stone cross when traveling by river. They named it "St. Croix" or "Holy Cross."

4   Learn more about Philadelphia Community Farm as their work evolves at https://www.buttermilkcsa.com.

5   Burial grounds. Minnesota Office of the State Archaeologist. (2019, June 21). Retrieved October 6, 2021, from https://mn.gov/admin/archaeologist/the-public/mn-archaeology/burial-grounds/.

Claiming Who You Are

1   Barry Holstun Lopez and Tom Pohrt, *Crow and Weasel* (New York: Sunburst, 1998).

2   Quinn Gathercole, "On Being Nonbinary," *The Wayfarer*, March 2021.

3   Catherine Gildiner, *Good Morning Monster: Five Heroic Journeys to Recovery* (Toronto: Viking Canada, 2019).

4   Heidi Barr, *Cold Spring Hallelujah* (Pawcatuck, CT: Homebound Publications, 2019).

Part Two

1   J. van der Leeuw, *Conquest of Illusion* (Wheaten, IL: Quest Books, 1996, first published in 1928).

Charting a Course

1   Mary Oliver, *Upstream: Selected Essays* (New York: Penguin Books, 2016).

NOTES

Observing the Wild

1   To learn more about We Are Wildness, visit www.wearewildness.com.
2   Douglas Wood, *Breathe the Wind, Drink the Rain: Notes on Being Alive* (St. Cloud, MN: North Star Press of St. Cloud, 2013).

Unlearning to Course Correct

1   Learn more about Charles Eisenstein's work at https://charles eisenstein.org.
2   This quote is often attributed to Kyle "Guante" Tran Myhre.
3   Ijeoma Oluo, *So You Want to Talk about Race* (New York: Basic Books, 2020).
4   Learn more about Happy Grizzly Adventures at https://www.happy grizzlyadventures.com.

Embracing Transformation

1   Philip Conners, "Beauty in the Burn," *Orion,* March/April 2015.

Dousing the Fire (with Love)

1   Anne Herbert, "Handy Tips on How to Behave at the Death of the World," *The Sun*, March 2019.
2   Paula D'Arcy, *The Gift of the Red Bird: A Spiritual Encounter: With a Guide for Reflection* (New York: Crossroad Publishing, 2007).
3   Visit chrislatray.com to sign up for *An Irritable Métis*, the biweekly newsletter from which this quote comes.

Rewilding Spirituality

1 A framework used by Christian explorers, first issued by European monarchies in 1493, to lay claim to territories uninhabited by Christians.

2 Kevin Johnson, "Expanding Our Minds: Recovering Contemplation in Pursuit of Wisdom," Carl McColman, Patheos, December 20, 2018, https://www.patheos.com/blogs/carlmccolman/2018/01/expanding-minds-recovering-contemplation-pursuit-wisdom/.

3 Mary Oliver, *Upstream: Selected Essays* (New York: Penguin Books, 2016).

4 Sam Gill, "University Presses; the Truth about Black Elk," *New York Times*, October 31, 1993, https://www.nytimes.com/1993/10/31/books/university-presses-the-truth-about-black-elk.html.

5 Black Elk and J. G. Neihardt, *Black Elk Speaks; Being the Life Story of a Holy Man of the Oglala Sioux* (Lincoln: University of Nebraska Press, 1961).

6 Suzanne Lindgren is the founder of Plant & Page. Learn more at https://www.plantandpage.com.

7 Rising Appalachia, *Leylines*. Track 8, "Sassafras." May 3, 2019.

Paying Attention in a Digital Age

1 David Treuer, *The Heartbeat of Wounded Knee: Native America from 1890 to the Present* (New York: Riverhead Books, 2019).

Declaring Your Place (in the Wild Family of Things)

1 Anna Quindlen, *A Short Guide to a Happy Life* (New York: Random House, 2000).

Becoming Older (with Faith and Hope)

1 Parker J. Palmer, *On the Brink of Everything: Grace; Gravity; and Getting Old* (Oakland, CA: Berrett-Koehler, 2018).

2 Mary Oliver, *Winter Hours: Prose, Prose Poems, and Poems* (Boston: Houghton Mifflin Company, 2000).

Tapping into Tragic Optimism

1 Personal health journals for any condition. (2015, December 22). Retrieved January 6, 2016, from https://www.caringbridge.org/visit/ evasaulitis/journal.

Accepting What Is

1 Land Back is an indigenous-led movement in the United States and Canada that seeks to return political and economic control of ancestral lands to the original stewards.

2 Clarissa Pinkola Estés, *Women Who Run with the Wolves: Myths and Stories of the Wild Woman Archetype* (New York: Ballantine Books, 2003).

Remembering What Was and Could Yet Be

1 Rachel Timoner, "The Holiness Hidden within the World," *The Sun*, October 2018.

2 SunRose refers to St. Francis as a "recovering boarding school." In the 1960s, the Catholic Church turned it over to the tribe, but SunRose said the boarding school mentality has been hard to change.

3   For more on the documentary *Women of the White Buffalo*, to learn more about the women featured, and to view the trailer for the film, visit https://womenofthewhitebuffalo.com.

4   To learn more about Dream of Wild Health and support its work, visit https://dreamofwildhealth.org.

5   I went to Luther College in Decorah, Iowa (a school and community that both celebrate their Nordic heritage), which is also the home of Seed Savers Exchange, a nonprofit that's dedicated to "keeping heirloom seeds where they belong: in our gardens and on our tables."

Seeing Wisps beyond the Horizon

1   Deborah Cramer, "Flight of the Red Knot," *Orion*, spring 2020.

Activating Hope through Grief and Gratitude

1   Interview in *O: The Oprah Magazine*, November 2000.

2   Megan Devine, *It's OK That You're Not OK: Meeting Grief and Loss in a Culture That Doesn't Understand* (Boulder, CO: Sounds True, 2017).

3   Levison Wood, *Walking the Nile* (London: Simon & Schuster, 2015).

4   From an interview via an event called *Wisdom Working for Climate Change* titled "On Grief and Climate Change."

5   Joanna Macy and Chris Johnstone, *Active Hope: How to Face the Mess We're in without Going Crazy* (Novato, CA: New World Library, 2012).

Becoming Earth

1   Arundhati Roy, *An Ordinary Person's Guide to Empire* (Cambridge, MA: South End Press, 2004).

Parting Words

1   Oriah Mountain Dreamer, *What We Ache For: Creativity and the Unfolding of Your Soul* (New York: HarperCollins, 2009).

2   Eva Saulitis, *Becoming Earth* (Pasadena, CA: Boreal Books, 2016).